Published by
www.elitepublishingacademy.com

All rights reserved.

No part of this book may be reproduced in any form by photocopying or any electronic or mechanical means, including information storage or retrieval systems, without permission in writing from both the copyright owner and the book's publisher.

First Edition Published 2022
© Shovelhead Dave
www.shovelheaddavebooks.com

Printed and bound in Great Britain by
www.elitepublishingacademy.com

A catalogue record for this book
is available from The British Library

ISBN Paperback - 978-1-915730-06-0
ISBN eBook - 978-1-915730-07-7

Dedication

This volume is dedicated to,......The Rats. That's right. Whether it's a nasty Rat Bike, a gnarly Rat Rod or a dilapidated Rat Car, these are the Rat Vehicles we love that transport us from Point A to Point B. Maybe our Rats are dependable and maybe they ain't all that dependable. That's all part of the fun and excitement of having a Rat and keepin' it goin' down the road, often times much to everyone else's surprise.

I also hafta mention the fine California folks that made this part of the Rat Life extra fun. From my original California ridin' partner, another transplanted Texan Oakland Steve (RIP) to California native Frisco Dave who is still with us and still ridin' to Kent & Lori, where ever they are today. And a special thanks goes out to the shop crew guys who were at Frisco Choppers, Dudley Perkins and Corvette Corner. All those wonderful shops are just special memories today, for those fun shops are sadly long gone today.

And last, I gotta give a special Rat Nod to the great state of California. As a snot nosed kid born in 1955 and raised in Dallas Texas, I had long wished to live in wild and crazy California, enjoying that west coast bike and car scene, and I finally got to do it in the 1980s. What a fun place California was to live and ride back then, before the helmet law. You wanna ride your Rat on Highway 1 and watch the sun set over the Pacific Ocean? It's there waitin' for you. You wanna ride your Rat through the Redwood Giants? They've been there hunnerds of years waitin' for you to come visit them. Whether you like gigantic tree lined mountains or flat hot cactus filled desert, crashin' rivers or big lakes, rolling farm land or the wine country, California had it all. I consider myself very lucky to have spent 9 years living in that great west coast state on the Pacific Ocean. I hope you enjoy this Rat Trip back to Rat Time.

Part 1: The California Rat Years

March 1983 to July 1988

To pick up where the Chopper Hobo left off,...imagine climbing on your show quality home built chopper at your friend's place on a fine Saturday morning packed doing an 850 mile road trip and by that afternoon you were riding a Rat Bike. Welcome to...The California Rat Years March 1983 to July 1988.

The road side repair on the busted frame is what kept me going, but the welding pipe on the frame sure burnt the shit outta the fancy Black Imron Paint and Red Pin Stripes, boo fuckin' hoo,...right? And by the time I got situated in the flat in the Haight in Frisco, the joy of riding a show chopper was now gone. There were three California folks in Frisco that knew the chopper from 1982 when it was still nice, and those three were Oakland Steve, James Perkins at Dudley Perkins HD, and Dennis over at Frisco Choppers, and he also rode a Shovelhead Chopper, a low-down mean Purple Chop which was probably one of the fastest choppers in town. All three of them basically said the same thing when they saw the 74 AMF Chopper, "What the fuck happened to your bike?"

To compound matters worse, James suggested I take the chopper over to the Blacksmith Shop on Harrison, and yes, I am still kinda surprised San Francisco actually had a Blacksmith Shop, but they did. And that fellow cut out a really rough big gusset and welded it into the neck under the original gusset for extra strength. I did not want it breaking again, right? So now it's even rattier than it was when I rode it into town, and that is how the California Rat Years gets off to a flashy start.

But what the fuck, right? At least I had a job now, took the toolbox to the job downtown in a Yellow Cab still I ain't got no car yet, but I have an idea to get back my old car back that I sold to my dad before I left Texas in early 1980. And if you think the chopper is a rat, wait until you see the car I drag back to Frisco from Dallas, when I say these were the

California Rat Years, I mean in every way possible. On days off I rode up and down Highway 1 exploring my new home. These photos here are of the 74 AMF Rat Bike in the driveway at Stanyan Street, California Coast, and another timed selfie and this time I shut my eyes, March 1983.

Part 2: The California Rat Years

March 1983 to July 1988

In 1983 Easter was the first Sunday in April,...the 3rd. To this working stiff now, that meant a 3 day weekend, yay! And Oakland Steve was chompin' at the bit to go ridin' and campin', while I kinda rolled my eyes at the idea, cuz all I'd been doin' was ridin' and campin' and I was kinda likin' to sleep in a bed. Hell, not only did I have a place to live in the Haight now, I even had cable TV, and that was back kinda in the beginning when only you old timers will remember how we used to pay a monthly cable fee and that meant NO COMMERCIALS on your fuckin' TV. My, how times have changed, eh? But wait, there's more. I also had this thing called "MTV" and they actually played rock and roll music videos back then. Who does that today?

So back to the campin' ride. Steve told me about a place up kinda close to Napa and Santa Rosa, a state park called Armstrong Woods, and it was out in the Redwoods. And there was a campground there called Ring Canyon Campground, not a KOA, but about the same thing. It was right in the middle of the big trees, and the camp sites had permanent piled rock firepits with grills for cookin', and they had wooden lockers to store your stuff in from the critters. And the main building had showers and a small grocery store. So we took off for it.

He said it was maybe a little over an hour's ride, which was nice for my road worn calloused butt from the past 18 months with no car, hah. Steve rode over to my place that Saturday morning and we did some big puffs and then kicked the two Shovelheads over and took off over the Golden Gate Bridge. We rode up Highway 101 until we got to Novato, then we peeled off onto Highway 121 on into Armstrong Park, which sits west of Napa.

We got into the campground and it was only 5 bucks to camp each night, and that included showers, so how's that fer a good deal, eh? And I don't mean this to sound any more corn ball than it is, but the next morning we found out they had a place up the road that rented horses, and since Steve and me were both from Texas,...umm,...why the hell not? So that Sunday morning we got us a coupla horses and went riding horseback through the Redwoods, up and down some pretty good size hills in the woods, and to this day, that was one of the coolest and funniest things I ever did.

We grilled T Bones on the fire pit Sunday night, grilled corn on the cob and taters wrapped in aluminum foil and baked in the coals. Although he didn't say much about it, I think Steve was kinda semi-impressed with the way I whipped out my mess kit and other cooking shit, and the way I could handle a campfire and cook up tasty vittels. Of course, Steve had a bottle of Jose and limes with him so we did shots of Ta-kill-ya and had some cold beers we got inside the camp ground grocery store. And I had the green bud. All in all, it was one helluva fun weekend, and was kinda like my Welcome Back to Frisco Campout.

Now about these here pictures, don't ask me why they turned out this way. Unlike today,...back then you never knew what your photos would be like until you paid some cash and got them developed. Maybe I was trying to be Andy Warhol-ish avant-garde? Maybe I was stoned and drunk? Whatever the reason, I got some strange photos from this trip, but I had to pay money for 'em so I didn't throw 'em away, see? So we got one front half of a chopper photo with road gear like maybe I was taking a picture of my jacket on the ground with the ocean and the ship in the background? Or maybe the camera went off too early? I dunno, hah. Then for some reason we got the back half of the 74 AMF Chopper, and then a coupla fuzzy photos camping in the Redwoods with that same ol' green and yellow Chopper Hobo tent I lived in up in Washington. And that's good ol' Texas/Oakland Steve (RIP) sittin' on the 74 AMF Chopper, one of the few people ever allowed to do that.

Part 3: The California Rat Years

March 1983 to July 1988

After the Easter Weekend ride and camping trip up to Armstrong Park in the Redwoods, life went back to sorta normal, as in, going to work and getting to know the neighborhood better. It was May now and I had the TV and phone and all them modern day corn-veni-ences going, so I was gettin' mostly civilized,...except for one more thing. I still ain't got no car or pick up truck. Bummer. I got no way to haul my toolbox yet, but I had met a coupla guys at work that turned out to be good pool shootin' and beer drinkin' friends, but I felt guilty imposing on them to haul my toolbox when we switched jobs. Carpenter jobs can sometimes last a few months or even a year or so, those are the good ones, but they can also last only a week, ya just never know.

The problem was I didn't want just any ol' car. I had my mind set on my own old car I had sold my dad before I left Dallas back in 1980. It was an old car that I loved dearly, even though it was a total piece of undependable rat shit. This IS a rat story, right?

When I was a kid in the 3rd and 4th grades, two things changed my life forever. The Beatles on Ed Sullivan and the new Corvette Sting Rays. I swore to my 8-year-old self that one day I'd own one. The Chevy dealer was only a few blocks from my folks' house and I used to ride my bicycle over there and stare at the sleek shiny Space Ships they called Sting Rays. The closest I came to having one was a slot car and a coupla models of them.

Then, in February of 1976 when I turned 21 and had my own house and the 74 AMF Chopper had the +25 over flame cut Girder on it, I decided to get myself a 21st birthday present. And you guessed it. I finally had my own 1963 Corvette Convertible. I got it from a cop in Irving Texas, where the Dallas Cowboys used to play. I paid $1,800 bucks for it and when my pop saw it, he was almost as pissed off at me as the day I first got the 1967 Sportster back in 1973. My dad simply hated motorsickles,... and now,... this shit? When he saw the 63 Sting Ray, he asked me "What on earth are you gonna do with that mess?" I said "I'm gonna restore it and make it into a nice car." He said "Good luck. You'd be better off turning a wheelbarrow into a car than that thing. Them Corvettes ain't good fer nuthin' except hauling snakes around." All these years later I still don't get what he meant, but that's the way it goes.

So here's what happened with the Rat Vette. When I was leaving Dallas I was gonna put the 63 up for sale. But, outta the blue, my dad sez he wants it. I was like,...........WHAT? He suddenly wanted the car, so I sold it to him for the same $1,800 I had paid for it 4 years earlier. And then I sold my house and rode the chopper outta Texas to Washington State. So after the 1981-82 Homeless Days ridin' around being a Chopper Hobo all that time, now that I finally had a place to live and a good job, I wanted that car back. So I called up my dad and he said sure,...he'd sell it back to me,..... ....for $2,700. That's the way he was, when I balked at the 900 bucks higher price he wanted, he said "they are worth more now." Umm,....yeah,......right.

So I sent my folks some cash to let them know I was serious about getting the 63 back, and I flew a one way plane back to DFW Airport. (Notice how all my 3 flights I ever took were always one way tickets? Weird, eh?) And then when I got to the folks' house and saw the 63, I nearly shit my pants he had taken a lot of it apart. I stayed to visit for a coupla days, scratching my head about this 63 Vette shit. Then it was time to leave. So now instead of the semi-dependable running car I had sold him, I loaded this rat turd thing into a U Haul truck along with its boxes of parts and I took off back to San Francisco.

The bummer part is I did not take the camera with me on this plane trip. But I do have this picture from when I first got it, and since this story is called the California Rat Years, it don't get much rattier than this ratty rat, right? And that 'hallway-pass note' is the back of the Irving cop's business card. He probably thought I'd get pulled over on the way home, eh? But I made it without any trouble. So here it is. Enjoy.

Part 4: The California Rat Years

March 1983 to July 1988

So in May of 1983 I had flown back to Dallas to retrieve the old 1963 Rat Vette from my folks' house. Since there was no way that turd would ever make the long ass trip from Dallas to San Francisco, once again I wandered down to visit the nice U Haul folks who were actually doing quite well with me renting their equipment alla time, hah.

My folks' front yard sat about 3 feet higher than their neighbors' driveway which had a concrete retaining wall on it. I backed the U Haul truck up into the neighbors' driveway with the back door facing into my folks' yard, opened the truck door, laid a coupla 2X12s down from the yard into the truck and I drove the 63 Rat Vette right into the truck. I had to squeeze out the driver's window cuz there wasn't room to open the door.

Next, I got some chunks of 2X4 from my dad's garage and I screwed down 2 pieces in front of the front wheels and 2 pieces behind the back wheels. That oughta hold that sucker from rolling back and forth on the 1,700-mile trip from Dallas to San Francisco which was gonna go through the desert. Then I threw all the other dismantled parts to the car inside the truck, slammed the door down, told everyone goodbye and off I went, headed west to the ocean.

While I was driving along the way staring out through the U Haul's windshield with nobody to talk to, my goofy mind started wandering like it used to do back then when I was headed down the road on a new adventure. My dad was a funny ol' guy. I had the ultimate respect for him and what he had gone through in his time. He was born in 1919 on a sharecropper farm in Dust Bowl Oklahoma and raised during the Great Depression. His own pop had died in 1933 when my dad was 14, leaving my dad as the man of the house, with his mom and four little sisters to raise.

As a teenager, my dad plowed the cotton fields behind horses and mules and he always told me how he smelled mule farts a lot, they sold eggs and pecans to make do. He used to tell me how he'd be out plowing the field and occasionally hear a Model T coming up the road and he'd drop the reins and run down to the fence so he could sniff the exhaust fumes when the car sputtered on by.

When WW 2 broke out he joined the Navy and was stationed out of Treasure Island and served his time in the South Pacific on the USS Don Marquis, which eventually sank under him one night during a battle. He had to abandon ship in the middle of the night. He also had to tread water all that night with the ship's fuel burning on top of the water while some of his shipmates were getting eaten by sharks. He treads water all night long and into the next day until an Australian ship finally picked him up the next afternoon. For the rest of his life my dad loved the Australians, and I do too, cuz without that Aussie ship coming by, I woulda never been born and coulda never ridden a chopper. So thanks to all you Aussies out there readin' this, wink, wink.

My dad also had his peculiar side, especially where I was concerned. He married my Oklahoma farm gal mom, as folks tended to do back then, and my carpenter dad built their little wood frame house in Dallas in 1949. And it was on this trip back to visit them that I found out what their mortgage payment had been. It was 66 bucks a month. Why does this matter? Cuz when I turned 18 and bought my first motorsickle, the 1967 Sportster against my dad's orders, he got pissed off at me sooo much, that instead of kicking me outta his house, he charged me rent,......25 bucks a week. Now let's all do the math. He was charging me, his 18 year old son, 100 bucks a month to live in his house where the payment was 66 bucks a month, he was the sly fox, eh? Making money off his own kid. Imagine somebody today charging their 18 year old punk kid more than their mortgage payment to live at home? Why,......lotsa folks would call that child abuse.

So anyhow, now ya know what all I was thinking about as I traveled along the journey westward. I made that trip in 3 days, stopping at road side motels two nights. It felt good and kinda strange to pull into the driveway on Stanyan Street in the Haight. Now it was my home away from home. But I wasn't done yet. I still had the Rat Vette to unload, but how,...and where can I do it? China Basin, that's where. The next morning, I unscrewed the 2X4s from around the wheels and then carefully drove the U Haul down to China Basin, which was an old semi-abandoned and dilapidated shipping district in Frisco. In other words, China Basin had seen better days back when San Francisco was still a blue collar working man's city with lots of shipping and trucking business, which also meant lots of regular blue collar guys working regular their blue collar jobs.

I eventually found a ramp that the semi-trucks used to back up to unload, and I backed the U Haul into the dock's ramp. I got out to check, and it fit perfect. I opened the U Haul's back door, climb in and wiggled into the Rat Vette through the driver's door and window again. Then I fired up that 340 HP 327, pushed in the clutch, put it in reverse and carefully backed the rat car out. Then I drove the noisy solid lifter Rat Vette down the ramp to the flat ground, shut it off, locked it up and drove the U Haul back to the flat on Stanyan to unload the rest of the car parts still inside the truck. Are ya still with me? After I had the parts unloaded, then I drove the U Haul down to Market Street and turned it in at the dealer there. So now I had to hoof it back over to China Basin and get the Rat Vette started up and drive it back to the Haight.

I got back to the flat and opened the garage door and drove the 63 Rat inside, pulled it right up next to the 74 AMF Rat Chopper which was still chained up to the post in the garage. See there? Now these two ol' Texas Rats are back together again, or should I say the three of us ol' Texas Rats are back together again, for the first time since 1979 in Dallas. Yay! I moseyed over to the Rat Chop and pulled a nice big fat roach outta the left side handlebar grip and fired it up, took a nice looong big deep drag and let them two rats get re-acquainted. After all, they had known each other since February of 1976. The next morning, I drove the Rat Vette to a hill overlooking the ocean and took this picture. Notice it still has the Texas license tag on back? So now I'm living in California with a Texas car tag and the 74 Rat Chop has a Washington tag and I got a Washington driver's license in my wallet.

Part 5: The California Rat Years

March 1983 to July 1988

Well,... the ol' 74 Rat Chop and the 63 Rat Vette got reunited in San Francisco in May of 1983. And now I finally had a car, or what was supposed to pass for a car, for the first time since September of 1981, yay! That means now I had a 4 wheel contraption to haul my carpenter tools around in. Now you might ask how in the hell could I haul my carpenter toolbox in this wreck? Easy,.....sorta.

Not only was it ratted out on the outside, it was also a rat on the inside. In other words, the interior was completely gutted out. No carpet, no door panels, no nuthin'. Just two wobbly ripped up seats rocking back and forth on the bare floorboard that weren't even bolted down. And get a load of this shit,..... no seat belts,.....GASP! Oh, the humanity! How illegal can ya get?

On regular days I'd ride the 74 Rat Chop to work in downtown Frisco through all the big buildings, fishtail pipes echoing off the concrete and glass canyons, but whenever I had to switch job locations or got laid off, I'd take the 63 Rat Vette to work to haul the tools. All I had to do was pull out the passenger seat at home and leave it in the garage, then pull the raggedy flea bitten holie rag top up from the back section of the deck. Getting the folding convertible top outta the back area gave just enough room to put the smaller top toolbox in there on its side. Then I'd set the bigger bottom toolbox where the passenger seat was supposed to be. Then I was set to go, but just remember,...no sudden stops.

Now for the good part. This Rat Vette ain't got no headlights cuz my dad took 'em out. Why did he take 'em out? I have no idea. But I knew they would be very involved trying to get them back in. The headlights were supposed to be hidden in the fiberglass headlight buckets which revolved with electric motors that didn't work anyhow, so I skipped on 'em for a while. Who needs headlights anyway, right? So, to get to work in the early mornings when it was still kinda dark, I'd take my two old 1960s chrome flashlights I've had since I was a kid in Cub Scouts and I'd turn 'em on and then stick each one in the hole on each side of the front end where the front turn signals were supposed to be, cuz the turn signals weren't in there either, then I'd wrap some duct tape around the lit up flashlights, jump in the Vette and off I'd go, and can ya believe no cop ever pulled me over for that funny shit even once?

Also, the windshield wipers didn't work. But if ya went fast enough, the rain would run up the glass so I didn't need wipers after all. Now do ya see why we're calling this part The California Rat Years? One thing that did work good on the Rat Vette was its Wonderbar Radio. The technical name for it was Signal Seeking Radio. It was AM only, and it had a vertical chrome bar on the left side and when you pushed that bar, the station indicator would automatically find the next station for you, kinda like an old juke box or in The Jetsons eh?

Meanwhile, back on the Motorsickle Front, I went to the Oakland Roadster Show and here's two Bay Area bikes that were there one, an Arlen Ness digger style and the other more traditional. And here's the front bumper and other chrome parts for the Rat Vette that I kept up in the flat so's I could polish the chrome at night after work while I watched MTV and had some beers and smoked that green bud, oh my! Ya see, all the chrome parts had rattle can gray primer on 'em, cuz back in the early 1970s the cop in Irving had sprayed the entire Vette with rattle can gray, even the front bumpers, grill, door handles, windshield wipers, back bumpers, rocker panels, if you can name it, he sprayed it rattle can gray, hah. What a true rat turd bomb.

On the fireplace mantle you can see the ol' orange and black Harley Beer Mug everybody used to have that I got from the back pages of Easyriders magazine and there is the ashtray shaped like a footprint in the sand I got at Daytona Bike Week in 1977. I used that ashtray for the green stuff back then. And yes, I still have both those things today and here's the two old chrome flashlights I used for the Rat Vette headlights, and yes, I still got 'em. Never throw anything away.

Part 6: The California Rat Years

March 1983 to July 1988

Didya ever wonder if old things with motors ever talk to each other? How many times have you been looking at an old bike and somebody next to you said "Man,...if that bike could only talk." Well,...maybe they do?

So what would it have been like when the 63 Rat Vette rolled into the garage in Frisco where the 74 Rat Chop was living? They hadn't seen each other since 1979 back in the garage at my little shacky house in Dallas.

After I left them alone, maybe it woulda gone like this?

74 Rat Chop: "Hey man! Long time no see. What the hell are you doing in here now?"

63 Rat Vette: "I ain't got no clue. Who the hell are you?"

74 Rat Chop: "I'm the ol' 1974 AMF Black Chopper that you used to live with back in Dallas, 1979, duh."

63 Rat Vette: "Oh, I thought I recognized your voice but I can't see you."

74 Rat Chop: "Whaddaya mean ya can't see me? What are ya,...... blind?"

63 Rat Vette: "Well,...actually,...yes. That old guy where I've been living the past four years pulled my eyes and teeth out."

74 Rat Chop: "HOLY SHIT! Man that sucks ass, so sorry to hear that."

63 Rat Vette: "I've gotten used to it now. So how's things been going with you?"

74 Rat Chop: "That Dave fucker that you used to haul around has been ridin' the shit outta me the past four years, that's what. He ain't even

got a car so I've been all he has to ride. What have you been up to, being blind and all?"

63 Rat Vette: "I've just been sittin' in the old guy's back yard all this time, no action, ain't been run in ages. I just sit there with no eyes or toofers, and the damn birds shit on me and there is this old Beagle dog named Bullet that keeps pissin' on my feet alla time. I only wish I had been as lucky as you and got out to put some miles in and blow the dust off, ya know?"

74 Rat Chop: "You'd better be glad you got a nice rest. You don't wanna go through the shit I been through the past coupla months, I can promise you that right off the bat. That Dave fucker rode me all up and down the west coast and back, rode me to Dallas and back and about wore me out. Camping up in the mountains was nice and all, but he also rode me through the rain and snow, not to mention extreme heat. Then up in Oregon a coupla months ago, he rode me until my fuckin' backbone broke,............in half."

63 Rat Vette: "Your backbone broke in half? Man, that's terrible."

74 Rat Chop: "I'll say it was terrible, and that fucker Dave wouldn't even let me rest for even one day. Ya know what he did to me? He kept riding me with my back broke, then he pulled off into some crummy road side clinic and had some goofy sawbones weld a pipe on my backbone."

63 Rat Vette: "That sounds just awful. I'm glad I'm made outta fiberglass and can't have nuthin' welded on me like that. Ha ha ha!"

74 Rat Chop: "Shut the fuck up, it ain't funny. And after the guy welded the shit on me then Dave raced some goofy white car down a mountain and made me go over 100, just a few hours after I got outta the hospital. Just look at my neck and see what them fuckers did to me?"

63 Rat Vette: "I can't see. I ain't got no eyes no more, remember?"

I'm just glad I wasn't there to hear all that bullshit and whinin', hahaha. So now these two Rats are in the same garage again and they get to ride around San Francisco. And speaking of Frisco, this is what it looked like back in 1983.

Part 7: The California Rat Years

March 1983 to July 1988

"The Blow Out"

The famous saying 'The coldest winter I ever spent was a summer in San Francisco' may not actually have been from Mark Twain, but it can certainly be true. Riding in drizzly San Francisco summer fog can get boring after a while, so in the summer months of 1983 I often rode over to the East Bay for riding, cuz the temps could be 10, 12, or even 15 degrees warmer. And that's where it paid off to have a good friend like Oakland Steve over there.

One Friday night that summer I rode over to his place and we were out riding around to some different bars, drinkin', tokin', shootin' pool, having a good time in general. And then before I knew it, bar closing time came. So, we rode back to Steve's place and I crashed there for the night on his couch. This marked the first time I ever stayed at his place without having the tent and sleeping bag involved, ha-ha.

Saturday morning, we woke up kinda sorta maybe even a lot hungover and Steve talked about this fantastic Mexican food place he'd been going to over in Berkeley that was open early for breakfast. He said their Huevos Rancheros was incredible and since I was from Dallas, I was very familiar with that breakfast. I loved it, crispy tortillas on the bottom, black beans, salsa, cheese and fried eggs on top. I was ready to go have some. But then Steve threw in the kicker. "You ever had Mexican coffee?" I sez "Nope, never heard of it." So Steve tells me how it's delicious strong brewed coffee with Tequila and Kahlua in it (imagine that with Steve?) and then they whip up some of that really heavy real cream and float it on top in the mug. Steve said it was kick ass for breakfast and he didn't hafta twist my arm, so we kicked the two Shovelheads over and took off for Berkeley.

Now here is where it gets a little bit fuzzy, cuz I do not remember the name of the road we went on, cuz I never rode on it again and I will never ride on it again. It is cursed. We started out from Steve's place close to the Paramount Theater, headed for Berkeley. The Mexican joint we were headed to was on Telegraph Ave just like most good stuff in Berkely is on Telegraph.

But to get there, we had to ride down this fucking piece of shit pothole filled curmudgeon of a shitty excuse for a road. When we were about two blocks from it sitting at a red light, Steve leaned over and warned me, "Now be careful and watch out on this road cuz it is really horrible." That shoulda been my first warning. When a guy who rides a swing arm and is willing to ride over anything tells you that the upcoming road is really bad, that should be like a fatal warning...right?

So, we took off from the red light and we approached the Road from Hell. It was a two-lane winding road and the right side north bound lane we were on had more potholes than anything I have seen before or since. There were nice big beautiful Eucalyptus trees everywhere which made the air smell great. And there were expensive houses all along the way, so why was the road so fuckin' horrible? The road zigged and zagged back and forth through the trees. If it woulda had decent pavement on it, it coulda been a wonderful ride. But......it didn't. Steve on his swingarm frame was riding maybe 35 or 40 miles an hour over the shit road, but I had to slow down to maybe 20 mph or so, cuz it was REALLY horrible. I had ridden cow trails in pastures in Ellensburg Washington that were in better shape, I shit ya not. Hell, in the early 1970s I was ridin' bulls in rodeos and the bull rides were smoother than this shit road.

That fuckin' road looked like bulldozers had been doing burn outs and drag racing on it...for months. So, I'm tryin' to dodge all the fuckin' potholes, but it was no use, they were everywhere. I'd lean right to miss one and hit another. My backbone was being jarred like never before. I felt like I was a tennis ball caught underneath a car just dribbling back and forth, non stop. Then it happened. POW!

The blow out. Oh joy, just great. I just thought I had it rough before, but now I'm riding on the back steel rim with the tire suddenly flat as a pancake on the rigid frame. I panicked, the back end of the chop was swervin' back and forth like crazy. I was thinking I was gonna crash, and if I woulda gone down, lemme tell ya it woulda been like sliding along a never-ending giant cheese grater. Somehow, I got the bike to stay under semi-control and got it over on the shoulder. With the motor still running, I feathered the suicide clutch pedal enough to get the bike to climb up on the little curb there on the side, and then came to a stop in the tall grass and weeds. Try that combination sometime, suicide clutch, flat tire, jumping a curb. There was a fairly flat strip of level ground maybe 4 or 5 feet wide before the big hill took over the landscape, going up into the big trees. Fuck, now what?

Meanwhile, Steve had no idea what had happened to me, cuz he was riding up ahead while I was falling more and more behind in the Pothole Hell. So I'm standing there next to the flat tire Rat Chop wondering what's next? Then I heard Steve's Shovel coming back my direction. By this time, I had started looking for rocks, pieces of solid garbage, chunks of wood, dead dismembered body parts, road kill squirrels, anything on the side of the fucked-up road to hold the back end of the 74 Rat Chop up in the air. Steve pulled up and nearly shit when he saw what had happened, hah. I managed to get enough rocks and a chunk of old semi rotten fence wood to make a nice wobbly pile of shit, so that I could lift up the back end of the bike and Steve helped me slide the back end sideways onto our pile of shit. It worked. The back tire was free and up in the air now. So, I unstrapped the tool bag and went in to work.

First, the bottom fishtail was blocking the right side of the axle so I pulled the fishtail off and threw it in the weeds. Then I took off the axle nut on the left side and then loosened the chain adjusters, moving them all the way forward, took off the master link on the chain, then pulled the axle out from the right-hand side and finally had a wheel on the ground now. Yay...big fuckin' yay. End of Phase 1.

Next, I asked Steve if he knew of any bike shops in this part of town. He thought for a second then said "Hell yes! There is an old Triumph shop on Telegraph, pretty close to where we were headed." I said OK, let's go there. I did not have the cable lock with me, plus there was nuthin' around to lock it up to anyhow. I had to leave the chopper sittin' there with no back wheel. Did not like that, but, nuthin' else to do. Steve kicked over his Shovel and I hopped on back ridin' bitch, and I held the rear wheel in between us and the sprocket side kept jabbing Steve in the back as we rode over all them fuckin' bumps and holes. Talk about a crowded fit on a bike? The two of us plus the wheel.

Steve rode us along the rest of the way over that bumpy ass piece of shitty asphalt that they had the nerve to call a road. And just before we got to Telegraph Ave, they had this big ass fuckin' tennis court school thing up on the hill on the right side, so any of you familiar with this part of Oakland and Berkeley might know this road from hell. We finally got to Telegraph Ave and pulled up in the Triumph shop's parking lot. Since it was a Saturday morning, they were kinda busy and we got a few strange looks from the hard-core Triumph guys as Steve pulled in with me on back holding the big rear Harley wheel. End of Phase 2.

Here's where I got kinda sleezy. We walked into the shop with the rear wheel, I plopped it down in front of the parts counter and I told the guy that I was from Washington State,.....with my Texas accent,.....and said I rode down here to California to visit my buddy Steve and just had a blow out up the road. And then I pulled my wallet out and showed him my Washington State driver's license for my 'proof', ha-ha. So there. It was kinda true,...right? Next, I told the guy I needed a new tire, mounted and balanced, cuz my bike was back down the road sittin' up on a pile of rocks in the weeds. Man, I wish like hell that I'da had the camera with me this time, but I didn't. Sad. It woulda made a funny ass fuckin' photo.

Those nice classy Triumph guys helped me out and told me they could have it done in an hour or so. That means that Steve and me snuck around the corner of their shop, had a coupla puffs of Steve's weed, then hopped back on his Shovel and rode off to have our Mexican breakfast and Tequila coffee after all. And I remember having three of them Mexican coffees, which were fantastic. Nice buzz with the weed thrown in, too.

Then we headed back to the Triumph shop and got the wheel with the brand-new tire. And this is where it paid off to be a Normal Citizen and have one of them plastic credit card things, cuz I didn't have all that much cash with me. Anyhow, after I paid the tab I went back to the mechanic that actually did the tire work and slipped him a 10 dollar bill cuz it ain't much fun changing a 16 incher, and I thanked him for getting me back on the road so fast. I never had the heart to tell these guys I was actually living in San Francisco now, end of Phase 3.

Steve kicked over his Shovel again, and I hopped on bitch again with the wheel in between us and Steve looked over his shoulder back at me and yelled "this time you keep that sharp sprocket pointed toward you" and we rode back to where I HOPED the 74 Rat Chop still was. I remember riding along all them fuckin' bumps holding that wheel that was jabbin' me now with the sprocket, until we got close to the spot where I thought it was, and,.....there it was, still perched up on top of the rock pile in the weeds, ha-ha-ha. Goody goody gumdrops as my grand ma used to say. Next, we put it all back together, got it back down off the rock pile and then got all happy again and we did another coupla puffs to celebrate. End of Phase 4.

Now as I wrote earlier, I do not have a picture of the 74 Rat Chop up on the pile of rocks, but I do have this earlier picture of it from before, and it is also in the Oakland Hills kinda close to where "The Blow Out" happened. And as you can see, that back tire is lookin' kinda bald-ish, hah.

Now here is where this picture really has me confused. Ya see, I keep all my old photos in dated order in the old timey photo albums. Yet this stage of the Rat Chop is confusing me. The photo is definitely from spring/summer 1983. You can see the big butt ugly gusset the San

Francisco Blacksmith welded on, so that means it is after March 1983. And you can see the bald tire on back so it was before the Blow Out of August 1983. But the handlebars are chrome and other photos of this time show the black bars. I mighta bought these chrome bars, put them on, then had their welds break as well and switched back to the black bars, who knows?

And now for the real ass kicker, I ran that wooden shift knob for maybe just a few weeks then switched back to the chrome ball knob. So this picture falls in between April and August of 1983, and that's the best I can guess. And that hill behind the bike is the one Steve and me used to climb up to go light up them joints, cuz we had a killer view of the Bay Area from up there. And just to assure everyone that I really do know how bulls ride, I was a rodeo bull rider back in the olden days and here is my 16 year old ass sittin' on a bull coming outta Chute #3 at the Kow Bell Indoor Rodeo Arena in Mansfield Texas, 1971.

I quit bull riding in 1973 when I switched to 2 wheels.

Part 8: The California Rat Years

March 1983 to July 1988

Having the August 1983 Blow Out over in the East Bay mighta been a scary thing that happened, but at least now I got a new back tire outta the deal, right? And there ain't nuthin' wrong with new tires. Next up was September and that month I got a call from my folks back in Dallas. My dad had a job as carpenter foreman on the new Lowes Anatole Hotel being built in downtown Dallas, which today they call the Hilton Anatole. Triumph Industries, the same company we had worked for at the DFW Airport back in 1973 was now doing the interior woodwork at the Anatole. My dad was starting to get up in years (like me right now, hah) and was getting ready to retire, thinking this might be his last job, and he wanted to know if I wanted to come work with him one more time. I told him of course I did. It would be an honor. So here comes the next road trip for the 74 Rat Chop.

I checked in with the construction company I was working for in San Francisco and they said it would be no problem for me to take off, their jobs were winding down anyhow, and they said to give 'em a call when I got back into town. So, I drove the 63 Rat Vette into work, loaded up and hauled my toolboxes back home to the Rat Garage where the Rats both lived.

Next up on the agenda was getting the tool box shipped there. I went to the Greyhound Bus depot and they said they could haul it for me as long as it was under 100 pounds. OK, sounds feasible. And the Greyhound Bus station in Dallas was only 2 or 3 blocks from my folks' house, so that was convenient. But that 100-pound limit meant I'd hafta leave the bigger heavier box at home and just ship the top box and work out of it. And that was OK cuz that's where my most wonderful delicate woodworking tools lived anyhow, like my razor-sharp Stanley planes and big long Greenlee mortise chisels and such. The bottom box was mostly heavier duty tools.

The last time I shipped the toolbox was from Wenatchee Washington down to San Francisco and that time I loaded them onto an 18-wheeler in a heavy-duty crate I made for it, outta 3/4-inch plywood and 2X4s. But with the 100-pound weight limit now, I had to think lighter weight shipping. Why am I wasting time writing about all this trivial toolbox shipping stuff? Don't worry, you will see.

Instead of the heavy-duty shipping crate, I came up with the idea of wrapping the toolbox in 1-inch-thick Styrofoam and then covered that in 1/4-inch plywood, got some aluminum angle for the corners and then wrapped it all in duct tape. You just can't go wrong with duct tape, hah. So, I got a fairly durable light weight method to ship it now...right? Well...umm......maybe? I loaded the packaged toolbox into the 63 Rat Vette and drove down to the bus station to ship it out.

But...nooooo. The guy refused to pack it on the bus cuz it weighed 104 pounds. I couldn't believe it, but their rules are their rules and if I wanna ship it with them I gotta play their game. So back into the Rat Vette the box went and back to the Rat Garage we went, up the big ass 17th Street hill to Stanyan Street where the flat was. I unpacked everything I had just packed and thought about it. Where can I lose 5 or 6 pounds to get under their 100-pound limit? Then...... BINGO! I know...I'll take out those 4 Jorgensen 12-inch Pony Clamps, my favorite all-purpose clamps. I can haul them with me on the 74 Rat Chop and that will be the end of that shit.

So, I packed the toolbox back up again and drove back down to the Greyhound station again and this time the box weighed under their limit, like 98 pounds or so, and that means it is good to go. So off it went into the bus with the suitcases......bye bye, toolbox, hope I get to see you again in Big D. So back to the Rat Flat I went in the Rat Vette. I started packing up everything I'd need for the road trip there. Not only will I need the tent and sleeping bag and normal road trip stuff, but also a few more clothes than I'd normally pack so's my dear ol' mom won't think her son turned out to be a pig wearing the same shit every day and I also had to pack my carpenter overalls and a work jacket just in case, and now I also got those 4 Pony clamps tagging along, so that is adding another 6 pounds or so to the back pack. I figured the trip would be about 1,700 miles and I might make it in 4 days if all went well, or 5 at the worst.

When I finally got everything loaded and ready, I told the two downstairs neighbor college kids I was leaving, offered them each a nice big fattie and asked if they could pretty please grab my mail,...what little there was of it back then. And since I was still single and didn't have any pets, I could be gone from this flat for a month or so and it wouldn't matter,...as long as the landlord got his rent check.

I remember riding the loaded Rat Chop down over to Haight Street and ate my last Frisco meal at All You Knead, ...pronounced all you need, like kneading bread... get it, ha-ha! It was a cool old hippie joint that served really good food and the little table I usually ate at had a fresh water fish tank with a frog in it and I always liked to watch that frog swim around. So I told the frog see ya later. After I ate, I told the waitress adios, stepped outside, fired up a nice big fresh fattie for dessert, then put it out and stuck it back in the left handlebar grip for later. Then I kicked the Rat Chop over and headed south out of Frisco. It was already a bit after lunch time so I was getting sort of a late start, due to having to pack and unpack and then re-pack the tool box, thanks a lot Greyhond, hah.

I rode I-280 outta town down as far south as Woodside, then cut over to Highway 9 on down to Boulder Creek. I rode a while longer after Boulder Creek and camped down by Bakersfield for the night. This picture here is at the gas stop in Boulder Creek, and check out that new tread on that new back tire. And yes, I am still flying that white and green Washington State license tag and this is without a doubt the most crap I ever packed on the Rat Chop in its entire 48 year life.

Part 9: The California Rat Years

March 1983 to July 1988

I woke up early the next fine September morning as I usually did camping out,... cuz the hard ass ground ain't all that comfy for sound sleepin' is it? I broke camp, rolled up the green & yellow tent into its carrying bag, folded the sleeping bag in half length-wise, then stuck the tent on the end of the sleeping bag and rolled the tent up inside the sleeping bag like a nice big burrito, hahaha. I'd also run a bungee cord through the center of the burrito and then that roll would sit on the front fender and the bungee would fasten to itself in the back of the wide glide. Now you know my secret for traveling with only 2 or 3 bungee cords, hah. I packed the rest of the shit back on the Rat Chop and got ready to take off on another day's ride acrost desert land.

My goal for this day was to make it to Kingman Arizona or maybe even a little bit further if I got lucky. The speed limit back then in 1983 was still 55 mph, so that kinda cut into the time situation, especially on roads out in the middle of nowhere that weren't exactly nice on rigid frames. I also did not wanna have any trouble with The Man out on road trips, so I kept the speed under control,...well,...as much as I could without having a speedometer, hah.

After riding into a little road side diner and grabbing some grub for breakfast, next I rode over to a service station and gassed up the Rat Chop and checked out the road map. Then I took off down a little kinda crummy Highway 58 to a town called Tehachapi which was up around 4,000-foot elevation at the Tehachapi Pass which is on the edge of the El Paso Mountains. I stayed on Highway 58 through Four Corners and rode on out into the Mojave Desert and rode through a little town called Hinkley and then headed on to the next town of any size, Barstow, where I could switch over to I-40 and make some better time,...hopefully. Sometimes the Interstates were smoother roads, cuz them little state highways could get in bad shape at times.

Gassed up again in Barstow and got an empty antifreeze jug out of the garbage can and cleaned it out good so's I could fill it up with extra gas, just in case I ran outta Ethyl push-mo-line out in the desert,...cuz that would most likely not be good. The next stop was Needles, waaaay the hell out there in the desert. And to get to Needles you ride through the Cady Mountains, the Bristol Mountains, and then the Devil's Playground,...interesting names, eh?

And that area is where this picture was taken. It's times like this that you hope you did a good job building up your home made chopper, cuz there ain't no convenient AAA Emergency Road Service, no smart phones, no GPS, and nobody else riding along with you to help,......gulp. And now the black handlebars are back on the Rat Chop for this road trip and so is the chrome ball shift knob. Too bad I didn't get another picture of the Rat Chop in the desert with the antifreeze jug on it, too, cuz it looked kinda like the Beverly Hillbillies going down the road.

Part 10: The California Rat Years

March 1983 to July 1988

Last chapter we left off out in the Mojave Desert riding along on I-40 trying to get to Needles and I had the spare gas antifreeze jug with me, which I had to use. Good thing I had it with me. There ain't much out there in the desert...back then anyhow. Maybe it's all luxury high dollar condos today, who knows?

Riding on I-40 East out there after you get through Devil's Playground ya get to the Providence Mountains and then into a little town called Essex with its elevation of 2,600 feet then you get on into Needles, and I made it there for lunch time. I pulled in to the first gas station I saw, filled up the tank and asked the guy if I needed the antifreeze jug anymore or would there be gas stations closer together out there, I still remember the older guy gave me a goofy look. Maybe he wasn't used to seeing choppers out in his part of the desert, who knows?

After gassin' up, I rode over to the nearest diner and ate. Don't remember what I ate so it must not have been all that great, probably a burger or hot dog. It's funny how some meals I ate out on the road still stay fresh in my mind 40 years later, like Mrs. Bromley's Dining Room, and the Mexican place in Taos New Mexico where I had my first Chicken Enchiladas with Green Sauce and that big pitcher of frozen slushy Margaritas with Randal on our trip back in 1979, or that cold ass can of Wolf Brand Chili on the side of the road after midnight in Colorado. On solo road trips I'd try to stop at the little independent places to eat, the mom & pop joints, but if there weren't any of those around, then Burger King or A&W would do. That's livin' high on the hog, eh?

After I ate in Needles and filled the gas tank, checked the oil and chain, it was time to do a big ol' puff and then head on to Kingman Arizona. Ridin' east outta Needles, I-40 takes a dip to the south and then crosses the Colorado River, then you get into a place called Topock and then I-

40 swings back to the north to Yucca. Next up is Kingman and I-40 straightens out to the east again, it was like riding a loop, which meant it took a little more time cuz it wasn't a straight line.

I had covered a little over 300 miles that day since I left Bakersfield and it took me about 6 hours to do it. So I decided to push on east and see how much further I could get. The elevation at Kingman is around 3,300 feet and the weather was nice so far, so I continued on the nice ride.

Then once again outta nowhere, I got to that stage where my mind was wandering while I was riding down the highway. I started feelin' kinda weird, even weirder than normal. I was not only taking in the spectacular desert scenery, but also taking in all the crazy shit that had happened to me in the past 2 years. That's what can happen when ya don't have anyone else around, you can get lonely and question things. I had sold my house in Dallas, had to live on that money when I lost my job, then had to sell the car to get by, then lost the apartment, lived in the tent and had to flop at friend's places in different states, and then I watched my only prize possession, my once beautiful show quality chopper, turn into a rat bike in one day. Not meaning to whine, but that was a sort of a lot to go through.

I now had a decent comfortable place to live in San Francisco. And although it was a crummy 63 Rat Vette, at least now I had a car to haul my tools and groceries. I had a good job in San Francisco and I was riding to a good job working with my dad in Dallas one last time. Compared to the previous year of homelessness, I kinda had it made, so why was I bummin' out here on the highway?

I think maybe I was just taking it all in, maybe having trouble getting used to the change of having a place to live? I know that might sound crazy to some people, but I think that's what it was. I can't speak for other homeless folks, just myself based on my own experiences. But here was the deal with me.....I got kinda used to being homeless, I guess. Think of it like this....take your front door key, for instance. You come to the place where you live, you pull out the key, unlock your door and you go inside. For 18 months I had not experienced that. When you have a place to live, you have a place to take a shower whenever you want, or use the bathroom, or go to the kitchen and make yourself a sammitch. Hell, you can even watch your TV or listen to your music if ya want, right? I had not had that experience for 18 months before. It took some getting used to.

And maybe what brought all this melancholy on once again was the fact I was sleeping in the tent again, and riding the same chopper down the highway again. I mean, it is the same green & yellow tent I was living in when I was living on the rivers and in the woods in the Cascades and it is still the same red sleeping bag and the same black AMF Shovelhead chopper...or at least it's a ratty version of the same chopper, hah. But 18 months of being a Chopper Hobo can leave its mark in your mind, sorta causing you too never really be sure of anything again. You just hope you don't lose everything again.

Some folks recover from homelessness sooner than I did, some take longer to recover, and some never recover from it. Not meaning to be dreary, but how many of us are just a few months away from being homeless? All it takes is to lose your job and miss a few house payments or rent payments and then it's suddenly 'welcome to the homeless club.' I felt like I had escaped being homeless, but not 100% sure yet. Anyhow, it was shit like that which was rattlin' around in my empty noggin while riding down the desert road cuz there was nobody else to talk to.

And dammit, I had accidentally left the Walkman and cassette tapes back home so I didn't have any music going now. Oh well. It mighta been Pink Floyd playing 'Brain Damage' with 'The lunatic is in my head' and that mighta freaked me out even more, ha-ha-ha. And then there were the times I'd go nuts cuz there ain't nobody to talk to. So I'd be ridin' down the road and start telling the Rat Bike some Texas Aggie jokes that it should know cuz it's also from Texas, and when I'd get to the punch line, I'd laugh out loud and then wait a few seconds, then I'd slap the gas tank and yell into the wind, "what's the matter? Don't you get it?"

I got out into the Juniper Mountains, out by a little itty-bitty town called Seligman, which was about half way between Kingman and Flagstaff. I didn't even get a camp ground that night cuz I don't know if they even had one around, that place was like a little abandoned ghost town.

I pulled the Rat Chop off the road and rode it out into the sticks a little bit, shut it off and just slept on the sleeping bag beside the chopper out there that night under the stars, didn't even bother to set up the tent. And no tarantulas or lizards or snakes or vampire bats carried me off, so that was good. Tomorrow would be another day and a fresh start.

This photo here is out there in the boonies. And if anybody wants to start one of them rock garden things, I know where there's a bunch of rocks out on I-40, and I think they're free.

Part 11: The California Rat Years

March 1983 to July 1988

September 1983: Didn't get all that much sleep the night before outside Seligman Arizona. I woke up right beside the Rat Chop and it looked like it was staring at me wonderin' if I was ready to go yet, so I rolled up the sleeping bag and stuck it back on the 12 inch over wide glide front end. Kicked over the Rat and took off back onto the highway, still on I-40 headed East.

There really wasn't any type of town around of any size the first half hour or so of riding, so I made it on to a place called Williams where I gassed up the bike and ate breakfast. On this ride headed East on I-40 I was gaining elevation, and Williams sits up there around 6,700 feet which meant the weather was cooling off a bit the higher I got.

The next stop would be Flagstaff which was just a short putt away now. And once I rode into Flagstaff, I saw an independent bike shop off the highway called Hopper's Hawgs. I stopped there and went inside and stretched the legs a little bit. It was a nice shop and I got one of their T Shirts to add to the bags on the Rat Chop,...as if I needed to carry any more stuff? I took a nice big puff and started off again.

About an hour and a half was Holbrook coming up, a few miles after Winslow. And after riding through Holbrook, the Interstate zigs a bit northward and you head out through Sun Valley and then by the Petrified Forest National Park, and the elevation there is still over 5,000 feet. Continuing on I-40 you go through some little towns like Chambers, Sanders, and Houck and you ride by the painted cliffs getting close to Lupton which is right on the New Mexico border.

The more I rode to the east, the cooler it got. I always liked to look at the population signs and the elevation signs riding through towns and cities, still do today. I find it kinda interesting, especially if nobody else is around. You can look down at the chrome rocker boxes on the motor and say shit like "Hey Shovel there's 4,320 people in this town and its elevation is higher than their population number." Gimme a break, sometimes it gets boring out there and the bike is all I got to talk to, hahaha.

From Lupton Arizona, I rode right across the New Mexico border. And now I had about 3 hours to make it to Albuquerque, which sits about in the center of New Mexico. And the closer I got to Albuquerque, the colder it got. Denver gets attention for being called 'The Mile High City' but ya never hear anything about how high up Albuquerque is, and it even sits a little bit higher than Denver does.

The main reason I was fixated on elevations back then is cuz the higher you rode, the colder it would get. In a car or truck, this wouldn't mean jack shit to anybody, but on a bike it's umm,... kinda important. And by the time I rode into Albuquerque, it was getting pretty fucking cold. And then the light rain started in. Luckily, I did not hafta ride far or long in the rain, cuz I got into town about the time it hit. So I grabbed a motel room for the night. All total I had ridden about 400 miles that day, not too shabby for a home built rigid frame chopper.

At the motel I took a shower and put on some clean clothes so as not to frighten the normal citizens, then I walked across the street in the cold rain to a fairly large restaurant that had a parking lot big enough for the semi-trucks to park in. And it was inside this restaurant that I got The Bad News. Big storm blowing in, cold rain turning to snow and possible freezing drizzle is headed this way. Some of the truckers who were headed west told me what I could expect up ahead and it was a big storm that could go on for a while cuz they just drove through it.

Holy shit. I started freaking out. Not to seem like a wimp, but during the past 2 years, I had kinda already had my share of riding in cold rain and snowy shit up in the Pacific Northwest. And here I thought I was getting out of it by riding to Texas? In the truckers lounge they had the TV screen going and they were showing this big storm coming, and it did not look good. I went back to the motel room and called my folks in Dallas to let them know what was up.

I did not wanna turn around and head back, cuz I'd consider that wimping out on the ride and then all the miles I had ridden so far would all be for nuthin'. But I also did not wanna ride through the shit and end up sliding off the road somewhere and nobody would even know what happened to my sorry ass, hahaha. And what if I did ride the rest of the way to Dallas and worked a few weeks with my dad,...then what? I'd hafta ride right back through the crap only worse cuz it would be later in the season.

The alternative was to turn right around and ride back the entire distance I had come so far, drop the Rat Chop off at the flat in the Haight, and then take a fuckin' plane back to Dallas. And my carpenter toolbox was probably either getting there right about now or maybe was already there at the Greyhound Bus station waiting for me to come pick it up.

Decisions, decisions, and I seemed to be fucked no matter which one I chose. My folks were even telling me to turn around and ride back to California, and they were wanting to see me, hahaha. So I made the decision to wimp out, turn around and head back to San Francisco the next morning,......probably in the rain, hopefully not in some snow. Ridin' in snow ain't as much fun as it sounds. This picture here is out there in the desert,....somewhere on I-40.

Part 12: The California Rat Years

March 1983 to July 1988

After making the decision the night before to ride back to California, I woke up in the motel room the next morning to cold drizzlin' rain, not good. Took a nice long hot shower trying to savor it all I could since I knew I'd be freezin' my ass off in a little while. Got dressed and walked back across the street to the truck stop cafe and ate breakfast and then sat there for a while drinking coffee with the truckers. The TV weather still showed the storm coming in. Shit. The truckers coming in from the east said it was still miserable and told me there was no way in hell that they would be caught dead riding a motorcycle in this shit. I said that's nice.

Damnshithellfuckpiss, hah. They were right, and that sucked. But what else could I do but get wet and cold today?

Well, no use putting it off any longer, might as well get to it. Walked back over to the motel room and took a look at the trusty AMF Rat Chop sitting there outside the room door, staring at me with its round headlight. Went inside and got dressed for the cold wet ride. That meant taking of what I already had on and regrouping with the long johns, jeans, t shirt and flannel shirt, jacket, flying ace leather hat, goggles and the heavy duty Ellensburg chaps, which I zipped down tight over the Easyriders Nasty Feet boots. It's not like I was gonna be waterproof by any means, but the extra road gear I now had on was at least better than nuthin'.

And now I felt like I was 40 pounds heavier than before breakfast, hah. Turned in the key to the room and the lady working the desk kinda looked at me like she mighta been thinkin',......'are you fuckin' nuts?' Loaded all the road gear bags on the chopper, kicked it over and took off into the cold rain. Oh joy. It's gonna be a fun day, fuck.

So now I'm riding the exact opposite of what I did the day before. What progress, eh? It looked like it was gonna be a fuckin' miserable ride back to Flagstaff, which was maybe 6 hours away, and it was. I was lucky the rain was not turning to ice or snow, so I kept my mouth shut, no whinin' to the Rat Chop allowed, after all things could be worse. This rain ridin' outta Albuquerque had some of them little tiny snowflake things mixed in so I knew I'd better get outta there as fast as I could. Staying overnight in the motel kinda let the storm get out west ahead of me, so now my punishment was to ride through it and hopefully outrun it and be back in the sun in the desert.

The ride went pretty well, for riding in cold rain anyhow. There wasn't that much traffic out there on I-40 West, just a few cars and 18 wheelers, which would throw up dirt water road spray all over the Rat Chop and me, hahaha. Eventually I outran the rain and kept pushin' on until I got to Kingman. And that was it for that day's ride. I got in almost 500 miles that day, so that was pretty good considering the weather. We'll see what the next day brings.

I got another motel room that night in Kingman and hoped the rain would peter out in the desert. After the shitty day of ridin' I did not feel like setting up the tent and sleeping on the ground right there and then. I wanted a hot shower, hot food, cold beer, stinky weed, and a nice warm bed to sleep in that night. Call me a picky bastard, I don't mind. So, I kinda wimped out again, big deal, hahaha. This rocky desert photo here is out in about the same location as the other photos were when I was headed the opposite direction the day before, hahaha, imagine that?

Part 13: The California Rat Years

March 1983 to July 1988

Woke up this morning in the motel room in Kingman Arizona, took a shower, got dressed, then called the folks back in Dallas to let 'em know of my un-progress adventure so they would know I'm still alive and kickin' at least. Back in the Olden Days before the Turnpike went in, the Main Drag between Dallas and Fort Worth was Highway 80. My folks lived one block north of Highway 80 and a coupla blocks from the Greyhound Bus station, and my dad said my toolbox arrived on the bus and was OK, not busted up or nuthin', so that was good. He said it was a really nice-looking toolbox, too fancy for working on construction jobs, hahaha. That was the first time he had seen it cuz I built it in Wenatchee in 1981. So now it made it back to Texas before I did. That ain't fair. I wanted to be there to show it to my dad.

After talking to them a bit, I went to have breakfast. Kingman sits at about 3,300-foot elevation so now I was getting back down off the higher land, which also meant things would be getting a little warmer now. My current main goal was to get back to San Francisco as fast as I could, stash the 74 Rat Chop back in the garage with the 63 Rat Vette and hop a plane to Dallas to go to work with my dad at the new Anatole Hotel they were building in downtown Dallas.

While I was eatin' and sluggin' down the java, I pulled out the road map to figure some things out. It looked like from Kingman to San Francisco was still a little over 600 miles. That would be a bit much to make in one day. If I averaged 100 miles in 2 hours back then on the rigid, that would equal about 400 miles in 8 hours and that was a good day's ride for me. 600 miles would be pushin' a 12 hour day riding. I might possibly make it, but then again I might not?

After I finished scarfin' down the breakfast and coffee, I hoofed it back to the motel room and loaded up the road gear on the chopper, checked outta the motel, kicked the Rat Chop over and rode over to the gas station to fill up the tank for the first time that day. I always tried to check the oil and chain first thing in the mornings if I could. Taking off from Kingman, reversing everything I had accomplished the coupla days before, I had to ride around that weird loop that I-40 does where it turns down south and then back northwest-ish to get to Needles, so that was gonna be the next stop. It was probably an hour or so away.

So I pointed the 21 incher west and took off out I-40 headed to Needles. No need to wear the heavy road gear today, cuz we were gettin' back to desert country, and even in September that area can still be kinda hot. And I never cared much for riding in anything over 80 or 85 degrees, that's sorta hot for me and the Shovelhead. And the trusty Shovel always seems to like the low 60s and even the 50s. That's when it seemed to run the best.

Now the Rat Chop and me were puttin' along down the road pretty good, tryin' to make some good time, ridin' along with the 18 wheelers. When I started gettin' close to Needles, it felt really warm to me, like almost too warm. I realized that when I saw the first gas station coming up. And I'd better get some gas and also look for a big plastic bottle or old anti-freeze jug in their garbage can, cuz next after the Needles gas stop, I'd hafta make it to Barstow. And Barstow was nearly 150 miles away and a little over 100 miles was about all my 1979 Paughco Mustang 3.2-gallon tank would handle. Them stroker motors gulp up gas a little faster than stock motors, so that was my predicament, hah. Moral: Make sure ya got enough gas to cross the dang desert, right?

So just as I'm gettin' into Needles and see the first gas station coming up on the right side exit, I was still feelin' really hot. Sometimes in the desert the faster you ride, the hotter you get. But this was not the case this time. I was slowing down to stop and still felt really hot. And what was extra strange was my back felt hotter than my chest. Hmm. Oh well, that's life in the desert, right? Maybe it was that hot fire ball up in the sky they call the sun, and it was beamin' down at me? So I pulled into the gas station and pulled right up to the vacant gas pump where there was an older couple with their motor home filling up on the other side of the pump I was at.

And as I was coasting up to the stop to shut the Rat Chop off, I noticed these really funny/horrified/shocked looks on both their faces, like they thought I was the first guy ridin' in a pack from a 1960s biker movie to tear up the joint. And still, my back was feeling really hot. And when I saw the looks on their mugs, I finally figured out that something must be wrong. So I turned around to see what was wrong, and what I saw was flames coming up my back. Yep. I was on fire. Imagine that? Oh great. Yawn. On fire and flames just blazing away, while I was sitting there at the gas pump, which was maybe 3 or 4 feet away, ready to blow up?

Well, when you catch on fire, I heard once that the first important thing you need to do is put it out, right? Right. So I started hittin' at the flaming duffelbag with my hands and then got the jacket free from the bungee cord on the duffelbag and then I used my 1975 AMF Harley leather jacket to beat the fire out. Hmm. That's better now. So the Rat Chop is sittin' there all nice and smolderin' and kinda stinky with smoke comin' up. Cool. I took the duffelbag off the back and saw the mess that I now had. Hmm,...again. The back seat is burnt up and the red lens from the Knight Light is all melted and so is the wiring to the tail light, brake light and running light. I quickly turned into the Rat Chop Detective and figured out that I musta hit a big bump out on the road which made the duffelbag bounce and wiggle down to the right side over onto the top fishtail and it musta rode there until it got hot enough to burst into flames.

My clothes are burnt up and now you can see where the previous story comes in about those 4 Pony Clamps that were too heavy in the toolbox. Remember when I said I had to take the toolbox back home and take out those 4 clamps in order to lose enough weight in the toolbox to be able to get shipped on the Greyhound Bus to get under their 100-pound limit? If anyone thought I was bullshittin' about that story, well, behold and take a gander at that cuz there's those 4 Pony

Clamps on the ground now with scorched handles, and even my black leather jacket and socks are burned up right there next to my old campin' mess kit, hah. Oh joy. It was hot enough out in that desert that I was not wearing the jacket, I had it tied on back on the duffelbag.

So next I gotta unload the Rat Chop and pull the tools outta the toolbag and go to work fixing the wiring on the back of the bike. That means I'm gonna be at this gas station for a while, eh? I always carry extra wiring and electrical tape and now that planning ahead is gonna pay off. And the nice old couple in the motor home next to me even gave me their now empty anti freeze jug so's I could fill it with Ethyl to make it to Barstow. How lucky can I get? And at least it ain't rainin'.

Part 14: The California Rat Years

March 1983 to July 1988

Well,...bust my britches,...what had started out to be a nice wonderful day puttin' through the balmy desert turned into a big stinky rat turd of a day, by catchin' on fire in Needles California. Now I had to get the Rat Chop,...which is even rattier now,....back to being road worthy, which meant re-wiring the back end of the bike at the gas station while the tourists and local onlookers looked on with looks of what appeared to be semi-shock with a bit of disgust thrown in. Maybe it was the smell of everything gettin' kinda scorched?

The main thing was I had to get the tail light and running light working again and that meant with no shorts, so I put in all new wiring with ratty electrical tape instead of nice soldering. So I kept to myself over on the side of the gas station and worked on the wiring. After all, I was gonna buy a whoppin' 3 or 4 bucks worth of Ethyl from then, so gimme a fuckin' break cuz I'm a high rollin' cash customer, right?

After I got the back end re-wired, I hid around the corner and took a big puff or three and then looked at what had happened to my cherished possession, the beloved contraption I had created with my own two hands and feet. Wow,... just look at it. What a fuckin' rat it is. Now mind you, in February 1983 this 74 AMF Chopper was a thing of beauty, a joy to behold, nice molded frame with slick black imron paint and red pin stripes, complete with a Joe Cox stroker motor and Andrews tranny build. Now this is September 1983 and just look at what the past 7 months has done to it. What a fuckin' cryin' shame.

From the February busted frame downtube and broken backbone on the road in Oregon to the emergency truck stop welded pipe fix, to the added San Francisco Blacksmith shop's big ass nasty welded gusset, to now this catching on fire shit out in the desert,...what a fuckin' disaster this chopper has become. And then it hit me,... what a disaster I have become again, hahaha. Back in February 1983, my carpenter toolbox was in a storage unit in San Francisco across the street from Dudley Perkins, while my boxes of chopper parts and other worldly possessions were up in a storage building in Wenatchee Washington and there I was, broke down on the side of the road out east of Portland. And I thought I had really 'improved' over the past 7 months, being a regular working stiff carpenter, paying the rent on time and shit like that, right?

So now look how much things had 'improved', hahaha. My carpenter toolbox is now in Dallas at my folks' house, my boxes of chopper parts and other worldly possessions are in the flat in the Haight Ashbury, and here I am once again, broke down on the side of the road at a gas station out in the fuckin' California desert with my road gear stuff burned up. That fuckin' shit woulda probably driven me crazy,...if I wasn't already crazy.

And now this fire crap has cost me even more ridin' time. So I made up my mind right there on the spot to try to ride straight through back to San Francisco. I wanted to take a shower in my own flat and sleep in my own fuckin' bed this night. Desert be damned, here I go off into the wide blue yonder,....whatever that is. After I filled up the Rat Chop with Ethyl and filled up the plastic jug the old retired motor home folks gave me, I kicked over the Rat Chop and was off again, out into the hot ass desert with all the other snakes, spiders, lizards, and rats like me. I probably had a 10- or 11-hour ride staring me in the mug. I'm off to do it non-stop now.

Out in the desert half way to Barstow, there is this road side Rest Area, out in the middle of nowhere. They had a water hose there and a phone. And the phone just hung there on a pole and it didn't even have a dial on it. It looked kinda like the Bat Phone down in Batman's Bat Cave. You'd just pick it up and it would connect you to Commissioner Gordon, or maybe some ol' lady bat at the local Sheriff's Office, who knows?

Anyhow, this photo right here is from that Rest Area. Once again, I set the timer for 10 seconds and jumped in front of the Canon, just so's I could show it to you nearly 40 years later. And I'm gonna let you in on a little secret right now. That Rat Chop and me stunk like shit, like burned up crap. It was sooo stinky it was funny. I shoulda captured that aroma and made a nice stinky perfume out of it, called 'Ode d'Road' and it would smell like burnt duffelbag canvas, burnt seat vinyl, scorched leather, melted plastic tail light lens, and burnt clothes. It coulda been a big smelly hit, who knows? And now about this amazing photo.....

That is not whiskers on my mug, that is sun burn, wind burn, and road burn with desert sand blasting thrown in and it hurt like hell. You can see where the back seat is burned to shit and the tail light is scorched. And I lost a precious bungee cord in the fire so now everything I got packed on the Rat Chop is now swinging from the front end. And how many times have people told us that you can't pack shit on the front end, hahaha? When I hear guys say that it makes me think they have never ridden a chopper cross country, that's all. So hey to them know-it-all bass-turds... guess what? You CAN pack shit on the front end of your chopper and ride it for miles and miles. I was riding down the highway doing 60 or 65 packed like this. It was not a fake set up pose for the camera. And don't worry, folks, stick with us here cuz it gets even worse.

Part 15: The California Rat Years

March 1983 to July 1988

At the so-called Rest Area out in the desert between Needles and Barstow, I took a little break to stretch the three legs and added the extra gas from the plastic jug. I had a really bad case of cotton mouth and not one cold frosty beer in sight. Bummer. So I pulled the joint outta the left handlebar, did another puff to make it even worse, then went over to the sun baked water hose they had hangin' there and sucked down some nice hot water from it. There. That made everything better. I still had around 500 miles to ride to San Francisco and I knew I'd be riding late into the night, thanks to the fire burning up the wiring on the Rat Chop...which is now even more ratty.

I kicked the nasty ol' Rat Chop over, pushed in the foot clutch, clunked the stick back into first gear, let off that suicide clutch with a bit of gusto and tire chirping, twisted the throttle and proceeded to ride out into the hot dry dusty desert. I still stunk like a smoldering fire. Big deal.

Once I got through Barstow I got over onto Highway 58 and took that to Bakersfield, where Buck Owens and Merle Haggard were from. Kinda desolate place to be from, eh? Reminded me some of Texas, wide open land and nice and hot.

After I got through Bakersfield, I kinda zig zagged and stayed on 58 until I got to a place called Buttonwillow and then caught I-5 there and rode north on that for a bit until I got to a place called Lost Hills and there I caught Highway 46 going west. Kept riding 46 and got into some hills by a place called Cholame which is a little bit over 1,000 feet in elevation, but it seemed like nice hills compared to the flat desert I had just ridden through.

I was stopping only for gas at this point, trying to make it back to Frisco even if I had to ride all night long, cuz I had just fuckin' had it with all the bullshit that had been going on the past few days. I got over to Paso Robles and turned north when I saw a familiar sign that made my cracked lips fuckin' smile from sun burned ear to sun burned ear. HIGHWAY 101! YAY! A familiar sign announcing a road I was familiar with, like I was nearly home,....almost. Still had 200 miles to ride into the night.

I stopped in at one truck stop and while I got gas I grabbed some eats to scarf down fast. Then I took off into the night again. I have no idea what time it was, maybe it wasn't even all that late, but I do know that I was gettin' tired as fuck. Maybe it was by Soledad or even up a bit further by Salinas, where Bobby McGee slipped away, where I started drifting off to sleep. Yep, that's right, ridin' along on a rigid frame chopper with straight fishtails and here I was, dozing off to sleep. Don't ask me how it happened, I still don't know to this day, hahaha. Maybe you've been there yourself?

All I know is I started yelling out to the wind, slapping my sore face, stretching my legs out back and forth from the foot pegs, reaching over with my left hand and pinching the shit outta my right arm, anything I could do to stay the fuck awake. I remember kinda dozing off then waking up as I was drifting back and forth in the lane with the cars and semi trucks still out on the road that night. And then? It happened.

Zzzzzzzzzzzzzzzzzzzzzzzzzz,.......zzzzzzzzzzzzzzzzzzzzzzzzz,.....

....
....

....
....

"HONNNNNNNNNNNNNNNNNNNNNK!"

That was the next thing I heard that woke me up as a loud ass alarm clock! Where the fuck am I? What the hell happened? The loud ass honking noise was the double air horn blast of the 18 wheeler that just whizzed by my head, maybe 4 feet away while he was doing 60 or so.

What the hell is going on? Where am I and what am I doing? Using my fingers, I tried opening my eyes which were glued shut with sand in them. I could tell I was a-layin' on my back, facing up.

I pried my eyes open and,....................

"HONNNNNNNNNNNNNNNNNNNNNNK!",..... again as another 18 wheeler rushed by my head, maybe 4 feet away. This time I felt the wind blow me and with bloodshot sand filled eyes I watched the Rat Chop shake back and forth on its kick stand as the wind from the semi blew it, too. I still can't figure out what is up.

My brain felt like it had a million cob webs in it, can't think. I soon realized I was there sleeping on the shoulder of Highway 101, with a ditch on the other side of me. I tried sittin' up and discovered I had been lyin' on my back on the shoulder of the road in the busted glass and little rocks and dirt with ants crawling all over me, HOLY SHIT! WHAT THE FUCK?

I slowly got to my wobbly feet, totally bewildered, brushed the ants and little rocks off me. I had no idea what had happened. To this day I do not remember pulling over onto the shoulder. I do not remember getting off the bike, or shutting if off or putting the kickstand down. OH NO! THE BIKE! Is it outta gas? Did I let it run all night until it ran outta gas? Is that why it ain't running?

Staggering the 3 or 4 steps over to the chopper, I reached out and pulled the gas cap off and looked down inside the tank and...........whew. It still had some gas in it. All this time, cars and trucks are still occasionally honking at me as they pass by cuz I'm still just about 4 feet from the edge of their lane where they are doing 60 mph or so. I was sleeping on the fuckin' highway shoulder. I still can't believe this one today. So what did I do next?

Why, I pulled the Canon camera outta the bag and took this picture right here. This is where I slept that night or early morning, whatever it was, right on the shoulder in front of the chopper. And don't ask me if that is the sun rising or the moon setting, cuz I got no idea. All I know is that is what happened. I was sore as fuck at this stage, it was hard to get my leg over the chopper and kick it back to life, but I did. I sat there on the idling chopper waiting for a clear spot to hit the road again and then took off on up Highway 101 North, headed to Frisco.

Part 16: The California Rat Years

March 1983 to July 1988

I got the shit scared outta me when I got rudely woke up by a semi truck's double air horns blasting me for sleeping on the shoulder maybe 4 feet off the right-side lane of Highway 101 somewhere out there by Salinas. Lemme tell ya right here and now from that awesome experience, the shoulder of a busy highway is NOT a good place to sleep or get woke up.

After I got up on my wobbly legs, kicked the chop over and got on it, everything kinda meshed back together again. So I pulled out onto Highway 101 and banged through the gears and got going again.

The first big ass truck stop I saw on the side of the road I pulled in. I filled up the gas tank, checked the oil and chain, and went inside and had me a huge ass breakfast, like a Lumber Jack plate, I stuffed myself cuz I hadn't eaten much the day before. I seemed to be more occupied with the smelly fire crap, fixing the bike to get it running again, and trying to make up for lost time.

I was very lucky I did not totally doze off on the bike and crash, and I was extra very lucky nobody ran over me while I was snoozin' on the shoulder of the highway. From Salinas I had maybe a coupla hours to go. I wasn't all that far away now and I kinda got pissed off at myself that I couldn't stay awake for the rest of the ride home a few hours earlier. No matter what anybody sez, I think sleeping in your own bed is much better than sleepin' on the gravelly shoulder of a highway with ants crawlin' all over you.

The closer I got to San Francisco, the thicker the traffic got. Since I was ridin' in on Highway 101 from the south side, that means I did not hafta ride over either the Golden Gate or the Oakland Bay Bridges, which also meant I didn't hafta stop cuz there was no line of cars waiting to pay tolls at the toll booths. So that was nice.

I finally got into the city and made my way up the busy streets to the Haight and got back home, right where I had started a few days before. What a miserable failed road trip that was. Three days out there to a big storm, then three days back catching on fire in the desert and what did all of that accomplish? Nuthin',...that's what.

I stashed the poor Rat Chop down in the dark garage with the 63 Rat Vette and took off by plane to go work with my dad. Since I was still single at this stage and didn't have any pets, it was no big deal to leave for a few weeks.

On the work front, I got to work with my dad for the last time before he retired and we did the woodwork in the lobby of the Anatole Hotel and we also did the woodwork inside their night club called The Crocodile Cafe, where we got routers and routed swirling grooves in the hardwood floors so the electricians could wire up the grooves with their strings of light buried down in the floor. That made the dance floor light up while the folks got drunk, danced, and tried to get laid, pretty cool, eh?

After 6 days of cross country ridin' fer nuthin', this photo here is the 74 Rat Chop back in the driveway on Stanyan Street in the Haight. And that brings us to the end of this part of the September 1983 Failed Road Trip Saga.

What's Up Next?

Meeting my new riding partner Dave in November and then getting hitched in December.

Part 17: The California Rat Years

March 1983 to July 1988

Now it's time to meet a new riding partner and get hitched, oh my. Yep, gonna throw in the White Surrender Single Towel and finally give up at the ripe old age of 28, which was the oldest I had been so far, wink, wink, hahaha. After I worked with my dad in Dallas one last time I flew on the big plane back to San Francisco, the toolbox got shipped back on Greyhound with no problem and I went back to work for the same company I had been at, but now on a new job with a different crew I hadn't worked with before.

The job was maybe 60% finished by the time I got there, still bare concrete floors but most of the woodwork was getting done. The boss man had me working on the big reception desk that was gonna be in the rich tenant's fancy main lobby just inside the elevator lobby. I don't remember right now if it was a law firm, stockbrokers firm, or some other type of legal crooks, but it was a very nice high dollar job, for sure. And my project was a big heavy reception desk kinda radiused with angled corners on each end that our company shop had delivered in four big chunks, two big heavy end pieces and two lighter pieces in the center, maybe 5 feet long each. It's a big desk for 3 or 4 nice reception gals to sit at.

I had to cut and fit the desk's base to the unlevel floor and prepare the big bottom part of the desk for the electrical, phone, and computer hooks ups in the bottom, which meant layin' those padded packing blankets down and flipping those big suckers back and forth to cut all the access holes until I had them just right. I was working on the big angled chunk on the right end when,............it happened.

The medium size pry bar that I was lifting it with slipped off and shot out from my hand before I could get the wedges underneath it. That means that whole 350-400 pound chunk-or whatever it weighed-came down on my left thumb, trapping it on the floor, HOLY SHIT! It hurt. And it held me there like I was a big rat caught in the rat trap. If you'd lay your thumb on an anvil and smack it with a hammer, that would hurt, but it would be over quick. This was more like slamming your thumb in a car door and it held you there, crushing you some more.

I could only do two things: 1... Wait for somebody to come by to free me which would be embarrassing, or 2... Yank that fucker out and deal with it. I chose Plan 2, and yanked my thumb out from under that big ass heavy desk. YOW! EXCRUCIATING PAIN!

I instantly went livid, mad as fuck and hurtin' like hell, so I did the only thing I could do now. I was on my knees on the concrete floor with my left thumb dripping blood cuz the little skin part end of it is still under that desk. So I had my hammer in my right hand and started yellin' and cussin' beatin' the shit outta that innocent floor.

"GAWDDAMN *SMACK* MUTHA *SMACK* FUCKIN' *SMACK* SUMBITCH *SMACK* ASSHOLE" like that kinda action.

Suddenly,......this guy I don't know pops his head around the corner, steps into the room lookin' at the insanity going on right in front of him and he asks "What's going on in here? You OK man?" So I held up my bloody thumb and he said "Oh shit, c'mon in here, we got a first aid kit." So, I followed the stranger into the other room where their gang box was and he got out the stuff and started wrapping my thumb up for me. It was pounding with every heart beat.

Then he sez "My name's Dave." I sez "That'll be easy for me to remember, cuz my name's Dave." He had on work boots, white Ben Davis coveralls and a black Harley T shirt. I had on work boots, white Ben Davis coveralls and a black Harley T shirt. So next he looks at me and asks "You got a Harley? I sez "Yeah,...do you?" He sez "Yeah,..I got a Shovelhead." I sez "I got a Shovelhead, too." Then Dave sez "Mine's chopped." So I sez "Mine's chopped, too."

And that's how we met. Since this was the end of November and rainy and cold in Frisco at that time of year, neither one of us had been riding our chops to work. Dave had been driving his Ford pick up and I had actually been takin' the N Judah street car, cuz it ran right in front of the flat at Stanyan and Carl Streets. All I had to do every morning was pack my lunch, go down the steps and out the front door where 2 or 3 bums would be sittin' and askin' for money before my boots even touched the sidewalk, and then I'd hop on the street car and it would take me downtown right to the front door of the building we were working in. I didn't even hafta pay parking, hahaha. It was a good system while it lasted, through the next few weeks anyhow. So that was the job front.

Now on the romantic front,...my 28 year old butt went out and robbed the cradle and got a 22 year old hard belly to get hitched to. Yep, that's right. I was now headed into what they call 'Domestic Bliss' hahaha. We did it in Golden Gate Park close to where the Grateful Dead used to play, kinda cool day but sunny for a change. Oakland Steve showed up with his New Main Squeeze to be on my side, while over on the Other Side of the Grass Aisle were the assorted hippie/punk rock critters that were associated with my new amore. We did it by our Favorite Tree where we got high and had our first date back in May of '83, a few months earlier.

'This chopper I made won't cross the ocean

This chopper I ride can't go to the moon

But I got an idea if you got the notion

This chopper I ride's big enough for two

....just me and you.'

So, we're moved in together and now I got twice the number of dishes to do. I was a professional dish washer back in 1967 when I was 12 years old making $1.00 an hour, so I'm experienced and really good at it and don't mind it too much. It's even calming for me, hah. But the thing I don't like is doing laundry. So now I got a live in laundry service, hahaha. But then I get this yammerin' in my ear like this shit: "Do you realize all you got for clothes are Levis and black Harley T shirts?" Me: "Oh no, my love. I also have that orange Harley T shirt from Richard Miller Harley up in Eureka, don't forget that one. Plus I got some white socks and skivvies and overalls and TWO leather jackets. So there."

And that's the way 1983 California Rat Year ended for me, with the 74 Rat Chop in the garage snuggled up to the 63 Rat Vette and two of us snuggled up in the flat upstairs, humpin' away like horny bunny rabbits. I had some boobs and tail to play the ol' Slap & Tickle with. Oh,...and we're still together. Never throw anything good away. This photo here is at the job where the desk squashed my thumb, but it was later when I was doing the wood pieces on the wall that would go in between the fabric covered panels the painters were covering, and there is a black Richard Miller Harley Davidson T shirt, from Eureka, California. And it looks like the bandage is already off my left thumb, so now it's probably just a regular ol' garden variety smashed black thumbnail, hahaha.

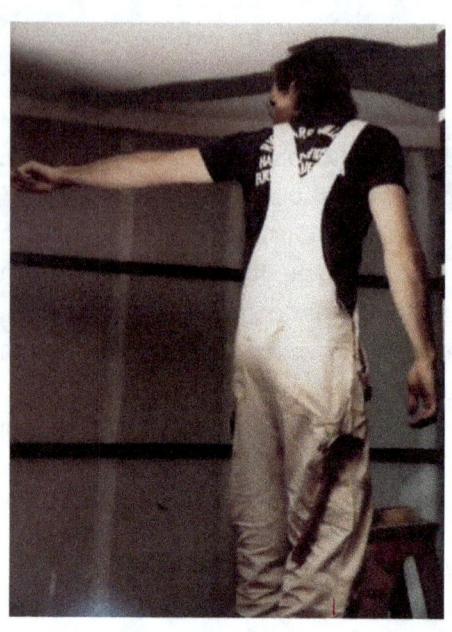

Part 18: The California Rat Years

Early 1984

1984 kicked off a little different than 1983 did. Instead of being homeless up in Washington State, I now lived in a rented flat in the Haight Ashbury, had a real bed to sleep in, a table to eat at, and a real shower. And instead of being free and single, I now had a ball and chain,...I mean,....I was now enjoying wedded bliss, and instead of having peace and quiet with the Icicle River running next to my tent, now I had two new lips constantly yammerin' in my ears, questionin' every move I made. So all was good now, right? Right.

On the job front, I had a decent payin' job as a sawdust eatin' carpenter and was working downtown with my new future riding partner Dave, the guy with the nice Ol' Yeller 67 Shovel Chopper. But Dave and me ain't been on any runs together at this early stage yet, it was still just mainly Oakland Steve I was ridin' with.

Meanwhile, down in the Bat Cave, aka the garage below the flat, lived the Two Nasty Grubby Rats. We got the ol' standard 74 AMF Rat Chopper down there and the 63 Rat Sting Ray sidled up next to it. Both needed attention. And at this stage, I had nearly given up on the 74 Rat Chopper. And I don't mean 'given up on it' like I was gonna sell it, no way, Jose. I fully realize that I am cursed with havin' that nasty thing til the day I croak. I know that,... and it knows that. This is a life long feud we got going on here, it vs me.

What I mean is, I had given up tryin' to keep the 74 AMF Rat purdy lookin', cuz,...what's the use? Unless you've built one of these blood suckin' money pit chopper monsters from scratch yourself, you got no idea how much time, effort, and money I put into that Nasty AMF Thing. All the sanding on the Bondo molding, the pro-sprayed Black Imron paint, the chrome work, the hot rod stroker motor and Andrews tranny that Joe Cox built for me the winter of 1979, all that time and work just plain went to shit. Its frame broke, it caught on fire, it wanted to be a Rat, so I let it be a Rat. Big deal. So what? Fuck it. It still hauls me to work. The motor ain't that old just yet, so it's gotta keep goin' no matter what it looks like.

I rode the Rat Chopper to work everyday unless it was pourin' rain, then I'd take the subway, cuz the 63 Rat Sting Ray was smokin' like the fires of Satan's Hell and the ol' 340 hp solid lifter 327 sounded like a billy goat chewin' on a tin can fulla plastic bubble wrap. It was ready to blow at any instant.

So,...enter Oakland Steve to the rescue,...yay! Now Oakland Steve had a friend our age named Craig who lived over yonder in Concord, and Craig's dad had an old friend his own age that had a garage out in Modesto, and that guy out in Modesto built good Chevy motors for hot rods out in the valley. So that's where I headed to. Modesto is roughly 100 miles from Frisco.

By this time, Oakland Steve was also doing better. At the start of 1983, him and me just had our Shovel motorsickles, that was it. We did not have a car between us. But by this time, Steve had a nice ratty old late 1960s VW Bug and I had the 63 Rat Vette. So off we go in our two cars, headed to Modesto. I'm drivin' the smoky old 63 and Steve is following me choking on the smoke, and he's also watching for spare parts in case anything falls off the Rat Vette. We made it out there. Steve drove us back in his VW and we were laughin' and firin' up the weed all the way back home.

A few days later, the shop guy whose name I can't remember called on the phone and said he had yanked the 327 outta the Sting Ray and went to work on it doing the machine work. The next weekend, I loaded up the duffelbag with the 63's headlight buckets and motors and lights and headed out to Modesto on the 74 Rat Chop.

'Headlight motors?' Yep. Them ol' mid 1960s Vettes had electric motors that turned the hidden headlights up and down in the front of the car. The later year Vette headlights were airline/vacuum operated, but these were still the old electric motors. So, I got to put the headlights in whilst the motor and radiator and its shroud were out, cuz it is mucho crowded in that engine compartment with them things in there. So I finally got headlights in the Rat Vette. But,......just cuz them headlights are in there don't mean they actually work, but they looked good enough to fool the coppers.

OK now what we got here is a picture of the 74 AMF Rat Chopper with my ass on it ridin' down the highway, and we got a photo of the 63 Rat Vette with no headlights at all, then we got a polaroid photo the car shop guy took and gave me after I got the hidden rollaway headlights mounted in there.

Part 19: The California Rat Years

Spring 1984

A few weeks later, eventually the phone call came from the shop guy out in Modesto. He had the 63 Rat Vette's 327 rebuilt to its factory 340 horse specs and it was fulla oil and antifreeze ready to come back home. Yay! That means all I had to do now was cough up some bread, and I don't mean the sour dough kind, it was the green kind he desired. If I remember right it was like 850 bucks or so for his machine work and pulling the engine out and sticking it back in. Kinda pricey back then but sounds kinda cheap today, eh?

So I made a call to my ol' trusty Shovelhead buddy Oakland Steve and asked him if he was free to give me a lift to Modesto the following Saturday, and he said sure, let's do it. The next Saturday morning he came by, I heard his VW Bug horn honk down in the driveway, so I grabbed us two fatties for the road and headed down the stairs and jumped into the Bug.

We did the 2 hour drive out to the valley, paid the nice guy off, then I jumped into the 63 Rat Vette and started back to the Bay Area with Steve following, just in case anything bad happened. Since it was a brand new motor build, I kept it around 50 mph most of the time, sometimes going up to 55 or 60, sometimes going down to 45 or so. The guy at the shop told me to do that, so's I wasn't just runnin' the new build at the same rpms all the way back home.

Now that the 63 Rat was back home in its Rat Nest Garage, the next few days I spent sanding on the fucker. Plan A was to get it painted that fall, if I could save up enough cashola. To help offset the expense of the paint job, I was doing as much body prep work myself as I could. Now I never claimed to be a good body man, but as a carpenter I had tons of experience sanding shit, hahaha, so I jumped right in and pretended the fiberglass body was just a big ol' chunk of wood I had to get done nice and slick. I'd spray some filler primer, then hit it with the long blocks, trying to get it nice and smooth. Filler primer, sand, filler primer, sand. You get the drift.

And here is one unusual thing I discovered about this ol' veteran of the drag strip Sting Ray. I was expecting to find 2 or 3 or maybe even 4 different colors under the Irving Cop's Drag Racing Primer, but once I got it sanded down, I found the original Mint Silver Blue color and,......................that was it.

Wow! This ol' drag race car had never been repainted, it was still virgin. And speaking of being virgin, the body had also never been hit. I guess it had spent most of its life just racing up the 1/4 mile drag strip. And now it has a brand new motor rebuild and the 4 speed and the rear end had been rebuilt in Texas in the late 1970s. Plus when my dad had the Rat while I was in Washington State, he told me over the phone how he did a brake job on it underneath our old oak tree when he put on the stock rims and tires and the exhaust system was also new. So mechanically speaking, the 63 Rat Vette was pretty sound at this stage. It just looked like a rat turd.

Instead of sanding the body in the dark garage in The Haight, I got to where I'd drive it out to Ocean Beach and sand it out there,......where I had me some beers and weed while I sanded. Why not? I had a spot on the beach where I had sanded a few times before. And then one day, the shit hit the fan with my sanding. Looked like a big storm was blowing up off the ocean. I figured I'd better get outta there. So I jumped into the 63, started it up, pushed in the clutch, put it in first gear, let out the clutch,...and,.....

.............the back wheels spun like half a turn and the fucker SANK in the sand down to where the frame rails were on the ground. Holy shit! And the storm is coming. I tried diggin' some trenches in the sand with my hands to see if I could drive outta the sand. Nope. No use. The frame rails still sat on the sand, the wheels just spun and spun, really slow-like. I pulled my t shirt off and crammed it under the back left wheel in hopes of gettin some traction that way,......nope, no such luck.

Now the rain is getting heavier. Maybe 200 yards away was a gas station/garage there on Highway 1 right close to the beach. I hoofed it down to the station and luckily, he had a tow truck, whew. Unluckily, when I asked him about towing me outta the sand, he said 75 bucks. Yikes! I said "Hey! I'm just right there",... pointing down the street to the beach to where the Rat 63 set. I sez, "All I need is for you to yank me outta the sand onto the pavement, I don't need to be towed 20 miles." Guys sez 75 bucks is his price, no squabblin' about it. Hmm. I need a Plan B, and the rain is picking up even more, hahaha. Great,...just great.

Next I hoofed it over and jumped my wet ass onto the underground subway, the N Judah I think it was, and that thing on train rails took me downtown close to where I had worked before. I got out underground and went up the escalator to street level, got wet some more, and then,...there it was! Awwright! My savior, the building for AAA Emergency Road Service. I ran in and joined them fuckers for like 30 bucks or so. They gave me a temporary paper membership card and I took the subway back out to the beach, it was still raining, ran into the same garage/gas station and showed him my new AAA card and now that guy had to pull the 63 Rat outta the sand for me for free. How do ya like them apples, Mister Rip Off? I made it back home,...finally. And by the way, I have never parked on sand again, wink, wink.

Meanwhile, on The Music Front, I knew this electrician at work that also worked on car stereos. I got a nice Pioneer Super Tuner and one of those graphic bar equalizers and had some tunes kickin' outta the back self-contained Pioneer 6 X 9 Coaxial speakers. I had extra speaker wire length on 'em so I could pull them up outta the back area of the car and put 'em up on the rear deck. We later took this 63 Rat Vette camping and them speakers worked just great. And since the Sting Ray didn't have any interior, just loose seats sliding around on the floor, I'd pull the seats out and take 'em down by the camp fire to sit in, like rockin' chairs. It was cool.

Then came the Fateful Day when the New Battle Axe and me wuz drivin' the Sting Ray down Haight Street and saw our old buddy Gary with his new main squeeze. They were walkin' east down the sidewalk like they were going down toward Market Street, so I pulled over and told 'em to hop in the Vette. They did. So now there's 4 of us in the Sting Ray, cruisin' through The Haight, hahaha. So whaddaya think happens next? If ya guessed flashing red lights, you guessed right. A cop pulled us over right by Divisadero Street.

He came up to my window and sez "You know why I pulled you over, right?" I played dumb and said "Nope. I wasn't speeding, was I?" He kinda laughs at me and sez "Did you know you have four people in a car that only has two seats?"

Then he bent over and looked into the car to see if we had any seat belts, and of course, we didn't. That cop was really nice, kinda laughed and shook his head and told us we can't have four people in this car. I did not argue with him, of course, cuz I was just hopin' he didn't notice we ain't got any working headlights and no bumpers on front or back and it's still got a Texas license tag on it, he let us go and I promised to take the junky car back home.

These pictures here are of Oakland Steve's and my Shovels over in the Oakland Hills. When we were in Frisco, we'd go up on Twin Peaks to get high. And when we were in Oakland, we'd go to this spot. Just up that grassy hill you could see forever, and we could still keep an eye peeled on the bikes. The other photos show the new stereo in the Rat Vette and the area by the windmill where I'd sand sometimes.

And whenever I'd hafta haul the carpenter toolbox to another job, you can see how easy it was to haul it in the Rat Vette. It's like a side ways pick up, eh?

Part 20: The California Rat Years

Spring 1984

At this stage the 74 AMF Rat Chop might look like a rat turd, but at least it was still mechanically sound, plus it had two new tires and a new chain, yay. It was just kinda ugly. So what? At least it still got us around and it never broke down on me. It was like a little dependable ugly puppy,......or ugly hog. And the 63 Rat Vette might be an ugly duckling, too, but at least it is now running solid as well.

Downtown San Francisco has entire blocks devoted to motorsickle parking only. Tons and tons of parking spots with meters for bikes to park in. I parked in those spots when I was at work. One day I came out to the chopper to find this note on the seat, tucked underneath the cable lock. It sez, "No need to lock. Nobody will steal this piece of shit." Now,..that ain't very nice, is it? I've kept that nice little note in the stash box all this time as a memory of fun days.

What we got here is some San Francisco Scenes from back in the Olden Daze. Lookie at them old cars! And there's the ratty ol' 74 AMF Chopper illegally parked nice and safe up on the sidewalk where it oughta be, and then we got a photo of the 63 Rat Vette with headlights this time and finally a shot that looks like it came from out of an airplane, but it's just the view from the top of Buena Vista Park in The Haight.

"Buena Vista" = Good View

Part 21: The California Rat Years

Redwood Run

Time for some Redwood Run photos. First up, here ya finally get to meet Ol' Yeller, the 67 Shovel that done-got chopped up back in 1977 by my work partner Dave, who's from the South Side of San Francisco.

Then ya got me standing in the parking lot lookin' kinda goofy and maybe or maybe not stoned just before we took off for Garberville, where the Redwood Run was held. And last, we arrived at the destination, Frenches KOA Kampground, nestled along the American River.

The area where everybody camps is called "The Pit." That's where the bands played, where they grilled our steaks and where ya got all your ice cold beer. Since they did not provide weed, we had to bring our own with the purple hairs in it. The Pit is also where all The Action went on, the slow race, weenie bite, wet t shirt contest, balloon toss, fun shit like that.

Part 22: The California Rat Years

Redwood Run

In these-here three photos you can see how the campground is laid out. Pretty nice set up, huh? Lots of tent area, the river is nice and cool if ya wanna jump in,..and I did a lot. I was an old river rat from livin' on the Icicle River up in the Cascades in Washington anyhow. So I already had me some experience with river livin', hahaha.

There's lot of space to park your motorsickle, too. And plenty of dirt, if ya like dirt. And the Hawgs run all day and all night, throwin' up some rooster tails, so if ya came here for some restful peace and quiet, ya might be disappointed a little bit.

Part 23: The California Rat Years

Redwood Run

OK,... movin' on along now. We got some nice clean wholesome family entertainment and fun motorsickle games goin' on here. Everybody,... man, woman, child and beast,... enjoys seein' purdy ladies who like to swaller and gobble them nice big fat wieners,...right? Right. So here ya go. Here's some nice wiener gobblin' to get ya goin' good today.

The trick is for the lady to ride up nice and slow on on the back of her ol' man's Harley and while he tries to slow down and nearly stop without his feet-ses touchin' the ground, the nice lady tries to gobble and bite the biggest and most-est weenie she can handle. And if the guy's feet touch the ground, then they are disqualified, the end, Game Over.

And the more weenie the lady can stuff down her throat, the better her ol' man likes it, see? He likes it best when she gets as much weenie down her throat as possible. And now lickin' the weenie and playin' with it don't count in this particular contest. She's gotta cram that weenie all the way down her throat without usin' her hands, see? So she tries her best to get as much weenie down her gullet as possible, all the way down to its bottom if'n she can,...kinda like Linda Lovelace used to do, if you remember her? Then the lady who swallers the most weenie is the wiener,...I mean,...winner,...and so's her ol' man.

OK, so much for that fun weenie suckin' contest, now for the next fun family game. These purdy young ladies in this next contest might not know what's gonna happen to them. I ain't quite figgered it out yet. Seems to me the young ladies were gettin' ready to do something, maybe they were gonna sing or dance, or do a jugglin' act? Anyhow, the ladies were just standin' there, mindin' their own bid-ness and then outta nowhere, these guys came up with these 5 gallon buckets of ice cold water. And get ready for it,.....the guys dumped that ice cold water over the ladies' heads! I shit ya not! The guys got them gals all wet an' stuff.

The water from the buckets went down the gals' heads and necks, got their hair wet, and then it drained down their shoulders, and next? It went down their chests-ses. And when it did that, it got their boobies all wet,...both of 'em! I could not believe it. And since the water in the buckets was all cold an' shit, that means it got their little cute nipple-things all hard and they stood up real perky-like.

And I think a lot of the guys in the audience saw them gals' nipples do that act. Cuz a bunch of them guys next to me started hootin' and hollerin' as if they liked it. Now the gals are still wet and their little nipples are still standin' up, and can ya guess what happened next?

Them guys came out with even MORE buckets of water and poured it over them purdy little gals. I don't get it. Were the guys tryin' to conserve the water at the campground and do the gals' laundry at the same time? Maybe so. Cuz next thing I saw, them gals started pullin' their t shirts off. Oh my. Maybe they were tryin' to dry 'em out or get a sun tan? Cuz I saw a coupla of the girls waving their t shirts in the air over their heads, like they were either tryin' to dry out their shirts or maybe chasing some 'skeeters away? I dunno. Anyhow,....that's what happened that day. Beats all I ever saw. They never had anything like that back at the First Baptist Church in Dallas. We just did regular dunkin' baptisin'.

Part 24: The California Rat Years

Redwood Run

Another shot from the Redwood Run Action. They say all good things must come to an end, and I suppose that means Redwood Runs, too, sniff, sniff. It's nearly time to kick our choppers over and head back to civilization and,.....work.

Over the following years, this became my favorite run to go to, until they changed its location, anyhow. Why they always gotta fuck with stuff we like and ruin it?

Part 25: The California Rat Years

Redwood Run

What Redwood Run would be complete without an Official Rat Bike present? Dave and me spent a little bit of time givin' this ol' Rat the good look over. As far as Rats go, it was very impressive. It's even got folks climbin' on it and it don't seem to mind one bit. That's Dave with the 67 Shovel Ol' Yeller on the right side, the guy holdin' them two beers and one of them beers is probably mine he's holdin' whilst I take the picture. I hope he didn't drink a bunch of mine cuz I need it.

I met the rat bike owner later and his name was Milo and he was from Oregon.

Part 26: The California Rat Years

End of the Redwood Run

Dave and me kinda started a tradition of our own at the Redwood Runs and probably some other folks did the same thing. Ya see, aside from gettin' all drunk and high watchin' the bands play and partyin' in The Pit at the run, what we also did at the Redwood Run was,.....get ready for it,.....we actually RODE our choppers through the Redwood Forest.

That's right. Now you might think that's kinda goofy to even say it, but I bet 95% of the 10,000 people who rode to the Redwood Runs never bothered to go ride through the Big Trees, cuz we never saw that many bikes in there. It was extra cool riding through the Giants, as they call 'em. It makes you feel kinda like a little ant or bug being in the shadows of trees that big and that old.

So here's ya a parting photo of a Redwood with a hole in it. I bet it's the first picture like this that you saw all day,.....right? And that was the end of this run. Now it's time to take down our tents, roll up the sleepin' bags, pack them on the choppers, and bounce along the 200 mile ride back home and go to,..... work,.....ugh. I mean, yay, I have a good job!

Part 27: The California Rat Years

Fall of '84

After the Redwood Run earlier in the summer, I kinda simmered down and kept working. And believe it or not, that brand new Neiman Marcus store I helped build back in 1982 was already doing some remodel work, so I got to go back to my old job site. Working on the nice showcases inside the fancy department store was a lot cleaner and easier than diggin' ditches for footings out in the dirt, lemme tell ya.

Workin' some OT let me save up some bucks on the side and down in the Rat Garage underneath our flat, I did some more long block sanding on the 63 Rat Vette. I was getting it good enough that I was nearly ready to take it in to the Corvette shop and get it painted back to its original color.

Here's some various shots of what was going on back then in San Francisco. We got a camping shot of the 74 AMF out in the Redwoods, the outside of the Neiman's job, a shot of the woodwork I did in their Rotunda Restaurant up on top, and a shot of Half Dome in Yosemite, and there's one of the Golden Gate Bridge I took while I was riding. Now you just got a grand tour and didn't hafta leave your seat.

Part 28: The California Rat Years

Fall of '84

Being a nice borin' stay-at-home newly hitched guy that was out working lots of overtime paid off,...literally. I got enough cash saved on the side to almost pay for the paint job on the 63 Rat Vette. So I made the plans with Rick Brown who was the owner of Corvette Corner in San Francisco to get the Sting Ray painted,...finally. The 63 was 21 years old at this point and this would be its first real re-paint,...if ya don't count the rattle can primer paint job from the Drag Racin' Cop in Irving Texas.

Corvette Corner was to the Vette folks what Frisco Choppers was to the chopper folks,..... THE premier shop to get high quality work done. The 63 Rat Vette certainly looked like an old dried up rat turd at this stage, but the tranny, clutch, rear end, dual exhaust pipes and brakes had already been taken care of during the previous few years, and the engine build was brand new, so mechanically it was sound. It just looked like a booger.

I drove the 63 down to Rick's shop and put it in line. Rick's shop was a big shop. He had a mechanical area doing repairs and service work, then he had the body shop where they got the cars ready, then he had another section for his paint work, then another section where they detailed the cars and did the trim work, interior stuff and soft tops. It was a One Stop Does All restoration shop, or a shop to set you up for drag racing, or whatever kinda Corvette work you wanted to get done.

Best of all for me was its location. Corvette Corner was down on the same street as the San Francisco Blacksmith shop. Rick's was on the corner of Harrison and 18th, and the 33 Ashbury-18th bus took me straight from Rick's shop to our flat on Stanyan. In fact, the 33 bus did a layover two blocks from our front door. This would come in really handy in a few weeks cuz now that the Rat Vette was in the shop, that meant I was back to just the 74 AMF Chopper for gettin' around town. And once the Rat Vette was painted, I would haul the bumpers and other chrome parts on the 33 bus down to the Corvette shop, hahaha. Door to door service. Anyhow, here we go with the final prep work on the 63 Rat Vette.

Part 29: The California Rat Years

"Ridin' Bitch" Fall of '84

One fun thing about ridin' the ol' 74 AMF all these years since 1974 is I kept the original throttle and grips all this time. They are kinda slick and shiny now but they still work just fine. And that also means the 74 Rat Chop still has its original Cruise Control. So, every so often I put it on Cruise and hop back on the back seat, fold my arms acrost my chest and just ride along like that for a while. It might be for a few miles or a few minutes, it don't matter to me none. And ridin' in a different position also gives the legs a break, right? Plus, the view is better from up there in the back. Is it legal? Probably not, so I don't do it in front of the coppers.

As you can see from the Speed Limit sign in the background, the limit was still 55 mph back then. But sometimes I'd stick it on 65 or 70 just for fun and I'd stay in the left lane and go passin' the cars and trucks in the right lane. I'd get some funny looks passing the cars while ridin' on the back seat and I could wave at the kids in the car with the funny looks on their faces. And if I wanted to switch lanes, all I had to do was wiggle in the seat a bit and I'd be in the other lane passin' another cage fulla citizen critters. It was like having power steering.

As for where this picture is exactly? I ain't got a clue for sure. But since there ain't no road gear on the front end, I'm guessing it was out somewhere on a Dudley Perkins H-D 1 day run, so maybe up to Napa and Sonoma if it was north of San Francisco, or maybe down by Monterey and Carmel if it was down south? Looks like Highway 101 to me with that funny double-double yellow stripe down the middle of the road.

As for who took it? I also ain't got a clue, hah. It's one of them mystery photos. Coulda been Dave takin' it from Ol' Yellow, or Kent and Lori on their Sportster or maybe Oakland Steve on his Shovelhead? All I know for sure is I'm toolin' down the highway havin' fun from the Bitch Seat. And no, I never got kilt doing this,...not that I remember anyhow.

Part 30: The California Rat Years

Fall of '84: Meanwhile, More Prep Work

Back on the 63 Rat Vette Front, now the pros are gonna fix everything my untrained eyeballs missed. But one thing to my amateurish credit, the guys said I did a pretty good job preppin' in the door jamb areas.

So now the professionals are gonna spray primer and sand and spray more primer and sand more until it gets just bee-yoo-tee-full and their arms are ready to fall off. It was a dusty situation, and every time they'd pick up the air hose to blow it off, there'd be a cloud of dust so big and thick you couldn't see through it. But that's the way it goes, the better the prep is, the better the paint job will be.

Part 31: The California Rat Years

Fall of '84: And Even More Prep Work, SIgh.....

I'm not the kind of lazy ass uncaring customer that just drops off a pile of shit work to get done and then never comes back by until it's finished. I'm the nosey type that's gotta be there almost every day after I get off of work cuz I like watchin' and learnin' how to do this stuff, see? And I know how to stay outta their way, so they didn't mind all that much,.....I hope, wink, wink?

And what I learned is how they spray the gray primer on, then spray a red oxide primer on the high points that stick up. That gives them the guide coat so's they can see exactly where they have been sanding and where they still need to sand more, and it helps to bring out the fantastic lines of this particular body style.

And then I can take the smarts that I learnt from these painter gurus and apply that new knowledge to my own chopper builds, see how that works? I get a free education out of the deal,...well,...it's sorta free, just as long as I cough up the $3,200 for this fine hand rubbed lacquer paint job at the Corvette shop.

These are the last photos of the ol' 63 Sting Ray in primer stage. That means the 63 Rat Vette is about to come out of its 12 year Drag Race Gray Primer Cocoon and emerge as one of the nicest 1963 Sting Rays in that town called Frisco. I got this 63 in Dallas back in 1976, sold it to my dad when I left Dallas in 1980, then bought it back from him in early 1983. And now it is finally getting some paint. Oh joy.

Meanwhile, the 74 AMF Rat Chopper is still gonna be a rat for a while, but now it's almost time for a nice Sting Ray to come outta this mess. And always remember these wise words,....."Never Rush your Painter or your Chrome Shop."

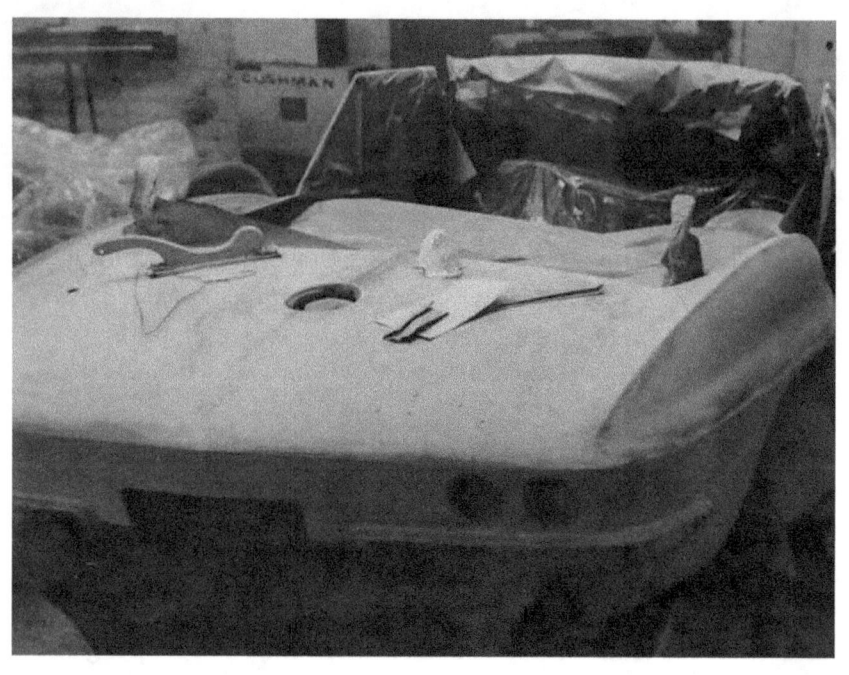

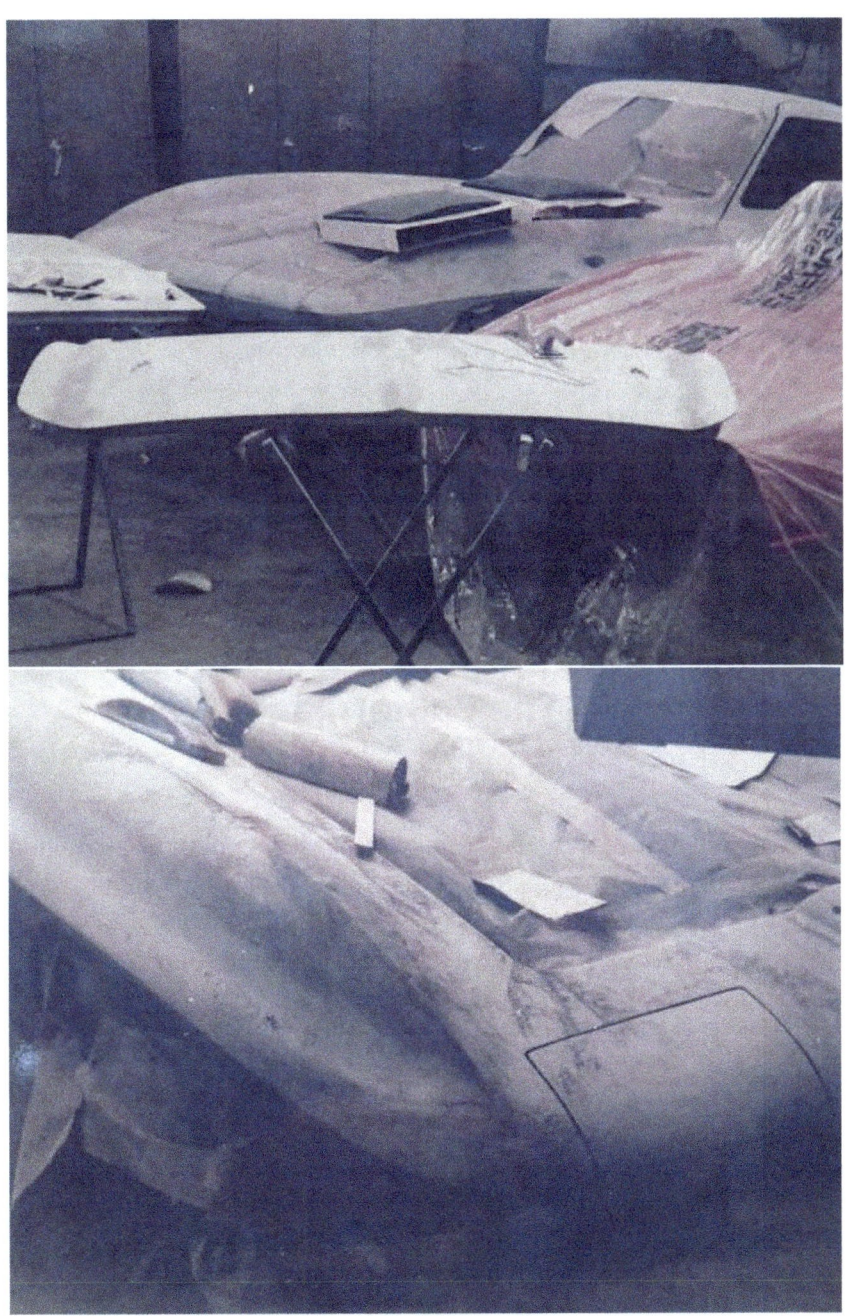

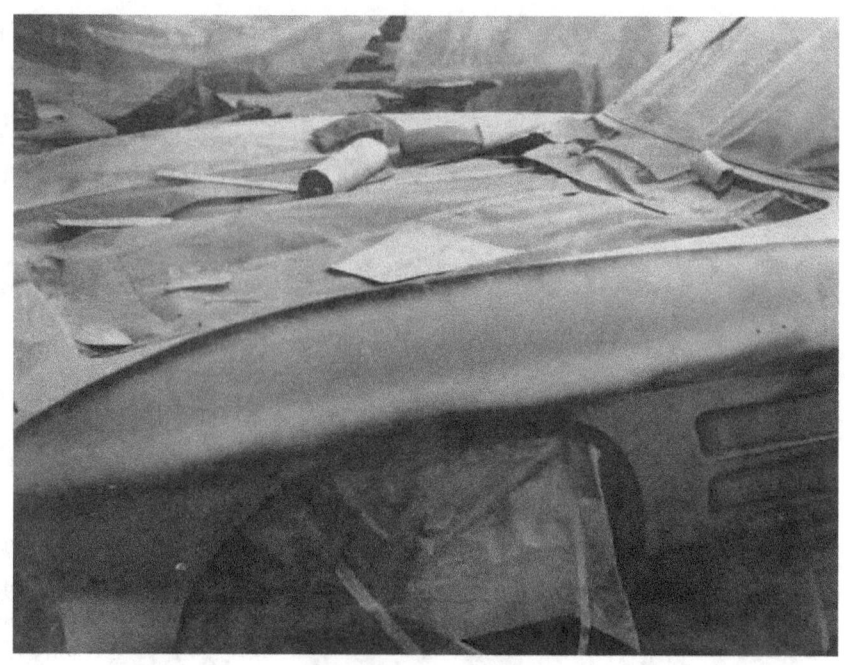

Part 32: The California Rat Years

1985 Rolls Around

So with the new year of 1985 comin' in, I'm still ridin' the 74 Rat Chop to work and meanwhile,...the 63 Rat Vette finally starts to get some color sprayed on its nasty ass. And this is gonna be kind of a long time-consumin' process. "Never rush your painter." Gulp. But it's startin' to look purdy nice.

Part 33: The California Rat Years

1985 We Discovered Roosevelt!

Raised in Texas and lived in 4 states and traveled in many more, and along the way I've eaten lots of tasty Mexican food throughout my entire life. But they all take a back seat to Roosevelt Tamale Parlor. (Doesn't sound like a very Mexican-like name, does it?) Rosie's dad loved Teddy Roosevelt so he named the place after Teddy and Rosie left it like it was when she took over. Enough of that, now about the food.....

Rosie had the finest Chicken Enchiladas en Salsa Verde I ever et, plus her Sour Cream Beef Enchiladas were fantastic. Her tacos and burritos were awesome but her biggest stand out specialty dish was her Chili Colorado. Succulent chunks of marinated tender beef and beans in her chili sauce. It was like eating delicious liquid fire, or hot molten lava straight outta the volcano, and it tasted soooo fuckin' good we just kept shovelin' it down our gullets every time we went and we had to hit this place at least once a week,...for years to come. Fresh made guac every time you walked in the door and home made chips and salsa, all in a dingy little place on Bryant & 24th, over in the middle of The Mission.

You can always tell you're in a fun neighborhood by the graffiti and the size of the steel bars on the windows, right? Right. I wasn't too worried, as you can see, I still got the cable lock around the headlight, so I wasn't too skeered. And when you are the only honky scooter trash inside with the neighborhood regulars, you know you found something special. When I'd park the 74 AMF Rat on the sidewalk out front, I was only about 8 feet inside the door, so it was no problemo por mi. How did we find this awesome and semi-hidden jewel of a Mexican joint? Rich on his Sportster told me about this place at work. And speaking of work where I met Dave on the 67 Old Yellow, the company we worked for actually had lots of fun riding partners.

Rich and Nadine were on a Sportster, Kent and Lori were on a Sportster, Brian was the original owner of his 1973 Moto Guzzi V7 Sport, and then Dave on his 67 and me on the 74 Rat rounded out the pack. Rich (RIP) eventually got killed in 1995 on his way to work when his Sportster hit a deer that jumped out on the road in front of him. And Dave was the first guy to find Rich dying on the side of the road. Big Bummer Times. RIde careful, folks. Be aware.

And now here is Roosevelt's Tamale Parlor,...which is also gone.

Part 34: The California Rat Years

1985 Sniffin' Paint, the Good Lacquer Kind

As the days ticked by, more and more paint got sprayed on the 63 Rat Vette. That Corvette shop was so big and had so many projects going on in there at once that sometimes I felt like the 63 Rat was like a lost needle in the Corvette haystack. But, there was progress.

At least the 74 Rat Chop was still dependable and running good, cuz I used it to get to work every day and even got groceries and likker store trips on the busted up thing. Here's a few shots of the Rat Vette paint job going on.

Part 35: The California Rat Years

Late Spring 1985

Ain't a whole lot to report at this particular time of 1985, we're still livin' in the flat in the Haight on Stanyan Street, the 74 AMF Rat Chop is still our only mode of transportation, the 63 Rat Vette is still in the Corvette shop down on Harrison & 18th Street getting painted...which seems like it's takin' forever, but the end result was worth it. "Never rush your painter."

So, for entertainment we'd ride the chopper around the Bay Area, ride up Highway 1 through Bolinas and that high coastal area where you are up riding on cliffs and look waaaaay down to the Pacific Ocean. We'd ride to Muir Woods where the Giant Redwoods are, and we'd ride on up to Mendocino County where they grow the finest you know what with no seeds. And sometimes we'd ride down south on Highway 1 to the Monterey and Carmel area, just toolin' around on the chopper which is almost free on the gas bill. Best way to see the California coast is on a home made chopper and it's also the cheapest and most-est funn-est way to see it, wink, wink. And we didn't hafta wear brain buckets back then.

Every so often we'd ride down to North Beach, which is the old Italian part of the City, or we'd ride over to Chinatown and mess around there some eatin' Hunan food and drinkin' their Plum Wine. And this photo here is from Broadway, where the night action was. Broadway is where the sailors would come party when the ships came in. Even my dad told me about these fun places that were there in business back when he was in the Navy and stationed at Treasure Island back in WW2. I'm sure all these fun places are long gone by now, and it's probably all high dollar condo shit.

Part 36: The California Rat Years

Spring 1985 Sprayin' More Paint

Now the hood is sittin' on the 63 Rat Vette and it's spray, then wet sanding, then more spraying, then more wet sanding, more spraying. It's getting really nice at this point.

And the paint guru's name is Mike that is doing the spraying and wet sanding. Some say the metallic colors are the toughest to spray. I do not know that from personal experience, since I am basically a black rattle can guy my own damn self, haha. And the color here is the original color for 1963, called Corvette Metallic Mint Silver Blue. And it was fuckin' beautiful, especially in the sun.

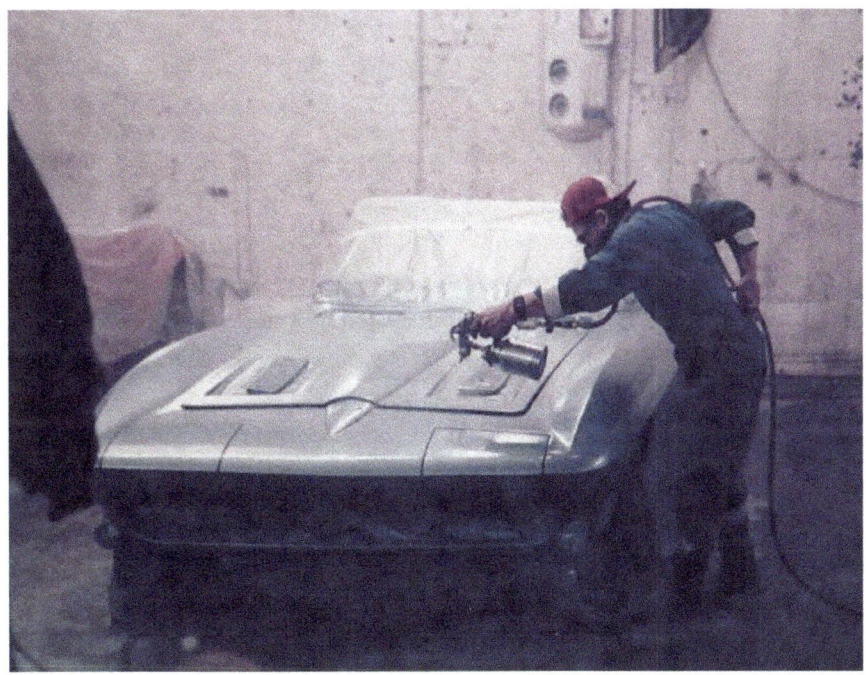

Part 37: The California Rat Years

Spring 1985 Gettin' Closer to Done

Next on the Rat Vette Front I had to clean up all these trim pieces which the Drag Racin' Cop has sprayed with gray primer back in the mid 1970s in Irving Texas. It was a lotta work, but I eventually got them purdy nice. Now.....how do I get them down to the Corvette Shop? The little pieces I stuck in a bag which I slung over the 74 Rat Chop headlight and delivered 'em that way...Chopper Express. As for the back bumpers?

Them suckers are shaped like boomerangs and wouldn't fit in the bag. So, I slung one over each shoulder and hoofed it 2 blocks down Stanyan Street and caught the 33 Ashbury bus, which dropped the bag and me off several minutes later right on the Corvette shop's corner of Harrison and 18th, perfect. I carried them into the shop, then came back out, hopped back on the bus going the other way back home and got the grill and the front bumper assembly. Now I'm carryin' some major big heavy pieces which are gonna take up lots of seat room on the bus.

This time I got some funny perturbed looks from the bus driver and other passengers as I was sorta bangin' their shins with the big chrome front bumper assembly gettin' on the bus. But,...what the fuck? I paid my fare so here I am. It mighta took-en me a while, but I eventually got all the chrome hardware for the 63 back down to the shop. They already had the door handles and locks there cuz they were on it when I drove the car down there back in the fall.

Meanwhile on the work front I was on a little remodel job in the old Mark Hopkins Hotel and that is the view I had lookin' down at the Transamerica Pyramid. Kinda looks like it was taken from a plane, eh? And the last shot is the last spraying of the 63 Rat Vette, just before it's ready to buff out and go back together.

Part 38: The California Rat Years

Redwood Run Time

So much for all that 63 Rat Vette shit. Now it's time for another little road trip to the Redwood Run. Yay! So let's pack the tents and sleeping bags on the choppers and head out on the highway.

Dave with the 67 Old Yellow Shovelhead and me got a tradition started where instead of meeting with the other riders at Dudley Perkins HD, we'd meet down in front of the Golden Gate Bridge. We'd do some puffs down there and then head on up onto the Bridge and take off for the run.

Ridin' to the Redwood Run was always fun, cuz the weather was usually perfect. And ridin' along Highway 101, sometimes we'd meet up with a bigger group of riders. We might be ridin' along with a group of 12 to 20 riders, or sometimes a big long line of a 100 bikes or so. And sometimes it'd be just us. Didn't matter none, we were just havin' fun riding the choppers up to the Big Trees.

It's about 200 miles from Frisco to Garberville where the Redwood Run was held, at the old French's Camp before they ruined it by moving the location,...in my book, anyhow. So, Dave and me would meet up around 10:00 on Friday mornings and head on up. Officially, the Redwood Run was a 2 day event. But Dave and me turned it into a 3 day run for us, cuz we liked to get there early on Friday afternoon and get the best camping spots in The Pit. So we'd always tell our boss we just HAD to get off that Friday. We had to pay an extra night camping fee for that Friday night, but so what? We're rich carpenter chopper riders, hahaha.

This time Kent and Lori were riding along with us on their Sportster. This was Lori's first time to go and she had heard the stories about how the bikes ride around all night long in the campground area and how sometimes a guy might be doin' donuts and his back tire might grab and launch him into a nearby tent. Shit like that can happen, ya just gotta roll with it, right?

So to be safe, Kent & Lori rented a cozy little cabin close by. Dave and me rode down to see them and I will admit it was kinda cool. Plus they got to sleep in a real bed instead of on the hard dirt. Cuz there ain't no fluffy grass in The Pit.

This photo here is a gas stop on the way up. That's Dave's bright ass Old Yellow Shovel right there at the pump and you can just barely see the front edge of the 74 AMF's front wheel over on the left side of the photo. I was there, honest. I even took this picture, hah.

Part 39: The California Rat Years

Redwood Run Time

Our little rag tag group of riders kept ridin' and puffin' and bouncin' and ridin' and puffin' and bouncin' until we finally made it the 200 miles to French's Camp, Whew. My back is still sore remembering how many bumps our rigid frames hit, hahaha.

Dave and me got there early before the main crowd and we picked out our nice tent spots over way to the left on this photo, cuz it is over by the Eel River that way. Any time I'd get to feelin' really drunk and kinda out of it, or if it got really hot, I'd go jump in the river, cuz I'm a river jumpin' kinda hobo dude. This photo shows the right hand side of The Pit. That's how big the campground was.

So, once we were parked and had the tents set up, now it is time to party, bring out the cold frosty beer and stinky sticky weed, I want my fingers gettin' REALLY sticky now. And if I remember right, they had Miller High Life beers at this one. And there's nothin' wrong with Miller High Life, it's the Champagne of Bottled Beer, right? At least that's what it sez on the bottles and cans.

Part 40: The California Rat Years

Redwood Run Time

Kent was a fellow carpenter that Dave and me worked with and he rode a Sportster. Lori was his sweet wife. She was 100% pure good gal and was an awesome cook. This is the little cabin they rented for the weekend.

Now they both had tickets and got wristbands to The Pit, so they could come and go and spend time with us there whenever they wanted to. But they were not camped there. So, Dave and me would take a break from The Pit Action and go ride over to their cabin and visit them for a few minutes and fire up some sweet green sticky buds.

The best thing about this cabin was it had pots and pans already there and dishes to eat on. And them two nice folks, Kent and Lori, went and got groceries in town and had Dave and me ride out for breakfast on our hungover "Sunday Mornin' Comin' Down." That's right, Lori made us all bacon and eggs and toast. And she had a nice big pot of coffee going and some of that Bailey's Irish Cream to go in the coffee. It was a very nice way to start the last day of the Redwood Run, lemme tell ya.

Part 42: The California Rat Years

Farewell Giant Trees 'til Next Year

So at the end of the Redwood Runs, Dave and me always rode through the Big Trees. After all, that's what it's all about, right? Unless you've been lucky enough to actually do it, it is kinda indescribable, but I'll try. The Redwoods are sooooo high and thick that you feel like a little ant ridin' through them. It is cool inside the Redwood Forest. The sun rarely breaks through. The clean air smells like nuthin' you ever smelt before. The forest floor is soft and spongy from hunnerds of years of stuff droppin' on 'em.

It is really quiet inside the Redwood Forest, except for the birds flyin' in the trees. And well,...except for when straight exhaust pipes from Shovelheads go blastin' through to add to the bird song mix, hahaha. It was really cool to get off the choppers and go walk amongst the trees there. It made us feel really small and kinda timeless. Them trees have been there since before America was founded, even since before Columbus landed here. Think about that one. The average Redwood Tree is from 500 to 800 years old. Does that make you feel young? And some of them are over 2,000 years old. That's almost as old as my cranky ol' mother in law was, wink, wink.

Anyhow, here's a photo of us in the Giants. The Shovel Chops are all packed up, ready to head back home and to work. And I do not have any issue with heading back to home and work, cuz at this stage, at least I had a home and a good job to go back to, if ya know what I mean?

That's Dave there by the 74 AMF Chop and that's Lori over by Dave's Old Yellow Chop. Now you can see why Old Yellow was always soooo easy for me to find when I was,...umm,....tipsy,... shall we say? And that is one big ass tree, and it ain't nowhere near the biggest of them. OK, now it's time to kick them choppers over and head back out of the forest to the highway.

Part 43: The California Rat Years

End of June 1985

The fun Redwood Run was over, the 74 Rat Chop was still dependable transport, but kinda butt ugly, and the 63 Rat Vette is still in the paint shop. So the Sweet Ball & Chain and me are out ridin' around on the 74 Rat Chop, just puttin' through the Haight Ashbury one fine weekend day after eatin' lunch. We decided to ride up The Big Hill in the Haight, up on top of Buena Vista Park. Buena Vista = Good View, see?

Buena Vista Park was always a great place to go get high, cuz you are already up really high, get it? So we rode the Rat Chop up to the top, shut the motor off and sat on some logs up there and pulled out the Sweet Doobers. From up on top of the park you can see the Golden Gate Bridge, Mount Tam, and the Pacific Ocean, all at the same time,...plus Golden Gate Park and all the multi-colored Victorian houses in between you and the sea.

After we spent maybe 15 or 20 minutes up there gettin' stoned, it was time to kick over the chopper and head back to the humble flat on Stanyan. The upsweep fishtails always sounded good up on top of the park, and they were barkin' off purdy good as we rounded the corner to start the descent back down the hill, when,.....

.................we both saw it at the same time. "Apartment For Rent" and it was on the coolest old building in the Haight Ashbury! There is a huge white stucco apartment building up there,...still there today,...and it was built around 1926 or so, if memory serves me. And it looks like a big ass Gothic German castle. It's a 7 story building and it just towers above everything else in the area. And it's got a For Rent sign on it?

Although we were both kinda lit up, and although we were ridin' on a noisy ugly Rat Chop, we pulled in anyhow just to see what's up with it. We pushed the buzzer and an older fellow came to the door and had us come in. Within just a few minutes, we discovered his name was

Bruce, his wife's name was Kay, they were originally from Hell's Kitchen in NYC, he was US Army under Patton in WW 2, and she was a teacher.

After the war, they had moved to San Francisco and they became the building managers of this apartment building. And now she took care of the paperwork for the tenants and he took care of the units himself, plus he was a Haight Ashbury artist now, did oil paintings and charcoal drawings and pencil sketches. He was sorta kooky, funny, and kinda beat-nik cool all at the same time and they both liked us enough to go check out the unit for rent. Guess which one it was?

If you guessed the itty bitty Penthouse up on top, you are the winner, hah. That's right. We had the chance to get the Penthouse and although it was a cramped apartment, it had THE most killer view you can imagine. But wait,...there's more. Are ya ready for THIS shit? It had an indoor parking spot that came with it, yay! So the Rat Chop and the Rat Sting Ray can both fit into the single parking spot. We struck the deal. 850 bucks a month and that included parking. That's a lotta bucks for rent back then, but so what? We were both working full time and I was gettin' some OT every so often, so we moved in on the first of July. And then to compound matters the Sting Ray was finally ready for me to pick up at the Corvette shop,...so I did. More about that in a moment. That was even more cash going out along with the first and last months rent, there was a lot going on this first week of July.

Since we didn't have that much stuff anyhow, moving was kinda simple,...after I rented a U Haul truck. So here's our new home, and we got that big plate glass window up on the top which was our living room, and the entire roof of the building is our "patio." There were 3 other little units up on top, but only ours had access to the roof. So back in July 1982 I was a homeless Chopper Hobo livin' in a tent on the Icicle River in Washington State, and 3 years later to the day, now I'm in a fuckin' Penthouse in the coolest neighborhood in San Francisco, hahaha. Imagine that shit?

Part 44: The California Rat Years

July 1985

Well now it looks like the ol' Chopper Hobo, former homeless tent dweller has gone rudy-poo candy ass and is now floppin' in a little hoidy toidy Penthouse apartment in the Haight.

Yep, we were livin' the High Life now,...with Miller High Life beer in the fridge. We threw a mattress down on the little hardwood bedroom floor, no box springs, no bed frame, just the mattress on the floor. Now that we had the Sting Ray back, I was able to go to one of those unfinished furniture places and got us two pine dressers. I coated 'em with clear varnish down in the garage, so now we are totally high class in the bedroom department.

As for the living room? We had two chairs and I took the old wooden box I used to build my choppers on, and that became our fancy coffee table, hahaha. Ain't that impressive? That's what we had sittin' in front of the big plate glass window.

The kitchen was so little if you took 2 steps you were out of it. And we had a little bathroom with a sink, pee pot, and shower, that was it. When you opened the front door to that apartment, you could take maybe 7 or 8 steps and that was it. But hey, it sure was easy to clean and chase each other around.

The 74 Rat Chop and 63 Sting Ray were safe and sound downstairs in the garage which had one of them fancy garage door openers on it. We just pushed the remote control button we had in the Sting Ray glove box and the door would open, just like the Bat Cave did when it saw the Batmobile coming up the road. We might take that action for granted today, but it was the first time I had seen and had one, very chic, ooh la la.

Then, 3 days after we moved in it was Fourth of July. We both knew they held the fireworks down at the Golden Gate Bridge, but we had no idea we'd be having such a spectacular free view of it all,...for only 850 a month, wink. Here's some photos of the new shack. This is what we came home to and looked at every day. Not too bad of a dump for a former hobo, eh?

Part 45: The California Rat Years

July: The 74 AMF Chop & 63 Vette

Rick had called and told me the 63 Sting Ray was ready. All I had to do was go down there on the 33 Ashbury bus, pay him a wad of hunnerds, and drive the Sting Ray back to our new apartment. So I went down there to get it. It looked fantastic with the paint all rubbed out and the trim pieces back on it. Hey, but wait a minnit. Somethin's missin' here. Where's the front bumper?

Oh,....that chrome thing that goes on the front to protect the plastic car's nose? Umm,......it's gone,.....somewhere's. Rick was in a pickle. Seems nobody in the shop knew what had happened to that front bumper. To this day, nobody knows what happened to that front bumper. It was just,.....gone. Maybe they bolted it onto another Sting Ray? Maybe somebody accidentally drove over it and smashed it and threw it away before they got busted? Maybe it got buried in a big pile of parts somewhere's? Maybe a UFO beamed it up? Who knows? Not Rick, and not me.

So I drove it home with no front bumper and Rick promised me he would go through his massive inventory of parts until he found a perfect bumper, not dinged up, not re-chromed, just a nice original one like I had. That was cool with me. Shit happens.

Here we have some photos of the Sting Ray with no front bumper and the new livin' spot for the 74 AMF Rat Chop and the 63 Sting Ray in the garage. Somebody still needs to get them bicycles outta there, and you can see my old Easy Rider poster I got back in the 1970s in Dallas. And I took one picture from up on the roof, looking down at the 63 parked across the street. Looks kinda tiny down there, don't it? And yes, the interior is still gutted, bare fiberglass floor, no door panels, seats loose, so it's still sort of a Rat Vette. And I blew sooo much cash this month that I ain't got enough left over for a new soft top yet, hahaha.

Part 46: The California Rat Years

Folks Visit?

July 1985 my folks in Dallas got a little motor home and they left with my Aunt & Uncle in their little motor home. The four of them drove all the way up to Anchorage Alaska. Maybe that's where I got my wanderlust from?

On their way back from Alaska, they came down the west coast and they stopped in at San Francisco for a visit, the only time they ever visited me anywhere I've lived. We had a blast. They had called ahead when they were still in Canada and we set it up so's they'd be hittin' Frisco on a Thursday. So all I had to do was ask the nice boss if I could be off work Friday and we made a 3 day weekend out of it.

I rented a big black Cadillac and picked them up at Ocean Beach. That was back when they'd still let you camp on the beach. You'd probably get arrested if ya tried that overnight campin' action today. I took them across the Golden Gate Bridge, which I guess wasn't all that bigga deal to them since they had just driven over it the other way. But when we crossed the bridge, I drove them on up to the top of Mount Tamalpais, which is the biggest peak north of San Francisco, elevation 2,500 feet. Sure, it was nuthin' compared to what they'd been seein' in Alaska, but it was still a nice clear view from up on top. I even drove them down to the Corvette Corner shop so's they could meet Rick the owner.

My dad and Rick hit it off just fine. While I had been up in Washington State, my dad had done some fiberglass and mechanical work on the 63 himself, even though he claimed he hated that 63 Rat Vette when I first got it, this car had been a joint venture with my dad and me, and now he finally got to see it in its original paint color. When my dad saw the paint job, he said it was the finest paint job he had ever seen on any car, and he was an old car guy from waaaay back.

While I still had the Caddy, I took them out for Mexican and Chinese food, sea food, Buffalo Chili, hit Pier 39, did the fun stuff. When it was time for them to go, I got rid of the Cadillac and drove the 63 Sting Ray down to Ocean Beach for the folks to see one last time before they drove away to their other adventures on the road.

My dad looked inside and saw the gutted interior was still the same and had a big laugh at my expense. He said "I see some things just never change" and winked at me. I told him if it was too fancy, he wouldn'ta recognized it. Here's three photos from that day and I'm adding an older one in primer from a few months before when we were camping, just so ya can see the nice lush ground California has to camp on, wink, wink.

Part 47: The California Rat Years

Fall 1985 Double No Front Bumpers

One day when I had been working up in the North Bay, I was drivin' home in the 63 and saw this other Convertible Sting Ray sittin' over by a light house. So, I pulled in and snapped this picture. Neither one of us got a front bumper on, hahaha. And as you can see, I didn't wanna pull up 'too close for comfort' and do any nose damage. After I snapped the picture, I left, so this Vette driver never even knew what had happened.

Part 48: The California Rat Years

Rick Finds a Front Bumper Yay!

Well, maybe it did take a little while, but after all, I am a chopper builder, and being a chopper builder means I gotta have patience,...right? Right. Good ol' Rick finally found a very nice front bumper for the 63, it was nearly NOS looking. And now it's on the Sting Ray and it looks just great. So here's some photo action, one up on the Peak and then two shots of the Haight Ashbury scene and now the 63 has a new white soft top, for the first time in many years, maybe since 1963?

Part 49: The California Rat Years

Late Fall 1985 Road Trip Time

Late fall came up and the Missus decided to take two weeks off work to fly back to Milwaukee and visit the Missus Folks. I was still bustin' ass on a law firm office job in a high-rise downtown workin' overtime, tryin' to get it done QUICK! Like 12 hour days, and we were nearly finished with the job, but not quite.

Worked another 4 days OT, got the job finished, then the crew got a lay off for a few days before the next job started, that's how the construction racket goes, eh? No biggie. And it was at this particular time that I had a decision to make. Go through the hassle of getting an airplane ticket, taking a cab out to the airport and flying off to Milwaukee and renting a car, blah, blah, blah, and listen to all the blabbermouth in-laws blabbin' for several days,...or go have some real fun of my own? Hmm.....

Started thinkin' of my ol' Chopper Hobo Daze pal, the Icicle River up in the center of Washington State, out by Leavenworth. I was wonderin' how the river and trees and rocks were doing without me now? I coulda taken the 74 AMF Rat Chop for the road trip back up there, but how many times must I repeat that action, hahaha? And then it dawned on me how I now had a 63 Sting Ray with new paint, new soft top and new engine sittin' down there in the garage with practically nuthin' to do. And since when did I ever take a road trip in a 1963 Convertible Corvette? Umm,....never.

So I pulled the trusty tool bag off the 74 Rat Chopper,...sorry ol' pal,....and I tossed it in the back of the Sting Ray, then I threw the tent and sleeping bag in the back end of the 63 and a few clothes and I hit the fuckin' road, and suddenly I realized I am now livin' out another childhood dream I hadn't thought about in years,...takin' a road trip along the California Coast in a fuckin' Convertible Sting Ray, ala the Beach Boys. So I'm off!

And this time I ain't doin' that fast I-5 shit by Mount Shasta, I'm ridin' all the way up Highways 1 and 101, right up the beautiful Oregon Coast. I ate clam chowder at the grottos along the way. And I saw this water fall falling straight out of a mountain on the side of the highway. So I parked the 63 just right, then I set up the Canon AE-1 on its side with the 10 second timer flashing, and I ran over and jumped in the car just as the camera clicked, hahaha. Of course back then, ya got no idea if the picture would turn out or not, ya gotta wait til your trip is over and go get the film developed. I was happy with the way this one turned out. It looks like I'm gettin' a free cold shower.

Part 50: The California Rat Years

Late Fall 1985 Road Trip Time

This photo here is taken holdin' the camera with my right hand way out to the passenger side underneath the rear view mirror and away from the steering wheel, drivin' with my left hand, hahaha, while going up the road and just barely getting the hood vents in the shot. Kinda lucky shot, actually. And that bridge goes over the Columbia River, which is the border between Oregon and Washington. A few more seconds crossin' the bridge and I'll be in Washington, yay.

I realize It ain't exactly a crystal clear photo, but it got most of the idea. I did some experimental 35 mm shots on this trip. So beware. Check out those hills, how brown they are this time of year in the "Evergreen State" eh?

And this time, here I am entering Washington State again, although now with a California drivers license and California car license tag, hahaha. That Washington State Patrol Officer Truman Douglas goon will be very happy to see me. But first, he has to recognize me in this 63 instead of being on the 74 AMF Rat Chop.

Part 51: The California Rat Years

Made it to Bridge Creek Campground

So here's the ol' 63 Sting Ray, made it to Bridge Creek Campground, which is the exact spot I used to live in the tent during the Chopper Hobo Daze. To those of you who have been payin' extra close attention to this drivel for some reason, you mighta noticed this is not the exact place where the 74 AMF Chopper leaned up against the tree by the tent. Why is that?

Cuz when I rode the Chopper back in there to set up the tent, I rode through the last legal camp site and then kept on ridin' on the foot trail another 50 yards or so, in order to get out of view from the citizen campers who would come camping on the weekends, burnin' up all the available firewood.

So where the Sting Ray is parked in this picture is right next to the trail head that I used to ride the Chopper on. But,...the tent spot I got is exactly where I lived before, right next to that nice little creek that was my fridge and kept all my beer and food cold. To get back in there to the same tent site, I just had to pack the stuff in a little ways. I left the car sitting right in this spot, parked in the trees.

Didn't worry about anyone stealing it cuz there wasn't anyone else there to steal it, and don't them headlights fit nice? Check out them awesome gaps goin' on there. And that is the other bumper Rick at the Corvette shop came up with, it looks purdy good, too.

Part 52: The California Rat Years

Meet the 1963 Rat Vette Seats

For some reason over the years, quite a few people seem to think that just because this 63 was a Rat Vette with a gutted interior, that it did not have any seats in it. They've asked me if I put yard chairs in it to drive around on, or milk crates, or 5 gallon buckets to sit on. Heck no, that would be illegal, you think I wanna get another ticket?

This 63 Rat Vette has its seats, but they were not bolted down is the only thing. I didn't want the seats bolted down, cuz I gotta haul my carpenter tool box in this ratty thing,...remember? And don't ask me if that is illegal havin' them loose seats in there, cuz it ain't got no seatbelts in it, either, or door panels. It's got a dash, and some of the gauges in it even worked, not all of 'em, but some did. The fuel gauge never worked, I always had to pull off the gas cap and look down in there to see how much gas was in the tank. And no, I did not use a lit match to look, hah. Oh, and it's got a stick shift coming up through the open hole in the bare fiberglass floor and that's all ya need to haul ass on down the road, right?

OK, now as you can plainly see in this ultra-excitin' photo right here, the same ol' green & yeller tent is set up in the same ol' spot it used to live in, right next to the same little creek and the same big crashin' Icicle River. All is well in the world now...temporarily, anyhow. I lugged them two seats down there by the fire pit. And I do think somebody else had been campin' in this spot since I was there in the summer of 1982, cuz the rocks in the fire pit looked like they had been moved around some. Try to fool me, will they?

With them two seats there now, I could lay acrost them sorta comfy-like and look up and watch the big ass moon and bright stars at night. There were quite a few falling stars and it seemed to me that there were a few more satellites than before.

But the river still crashed the same and the air was still nice and fresh,.......until I fired up the hand rolled smoky things. Then the air smelt even better. Now it's time for some hot dogs on the camp fire, cuz that's livin' high on the Hawg,...except the 74 Hawg is back home in the garage, sniff, sniff. Now I wished it was here with me. And I guess there won't be any of that fun Wang Dang Sweet Poontang action tonight,..... unless I can catch a slow fat squirrel or one of them horny she-bears

Part 53: The California Rat Years

Rat Vette Campin' on the Icicle River

Here's three shots of my favorite place to live, the Icicle River

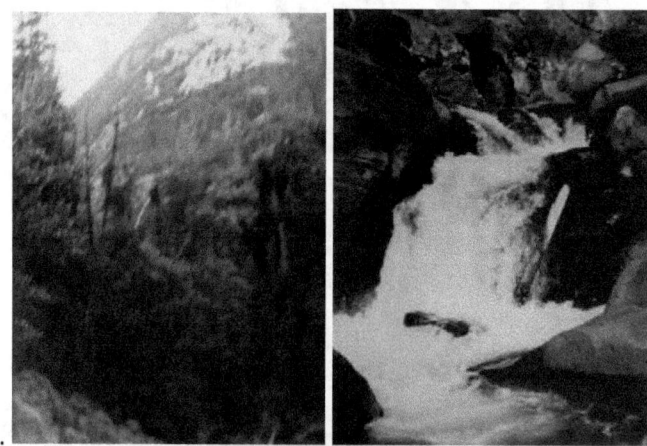

Part 54: The California Rat Years

My Old Cold Ass Swimmin' Hole

I guaran-gawd-damn-tee ya, if you jump into this Icicle River, your sphincter will be at the back of your throat in less than a heart beat.

How do I know that? From lots and lots of experience, bwahaha. When I was homeless livin' in the tent here, I'd jump in this ragin' water to get clean. And it's amazin' how fast you can get clean when the water is 32.0000000001 degrees, wink, wink. Most of the time, I'd be squeaky clean in less than 30 seconds,...honest.

They don't call it the Icicle River fer nuthin', it is pure melted snow crashin' over granite rocks and boulders as big as cars, buses, and houses. It is also loud,...very loud. And it likes for you to smoke lots of devil weed in it.

Part 55: The California Rat Years

About Time to Head Outta Camp

Here's one last shot of the Cascade Mountains, aka Heaven, before it's time to roll up the tent and sleepin' bag, stuff 'em in the back end of the 63 Rat Vette and head back to what they mistakenly call civilization.

After I rolled outta the crunchy gravel campground, I pointed the Sting Ray Nose down Icicle River Road and drove along next to the crashin' Icicle River for the last time. Then I stopped in Leavenworth one last time to eat at the German place on the triangle corner where I had Bratwursts and Sauerkraut with nice hot German Mustard, the bottle with the little German guy on it, and warm German Potato Salad on the side, yum, yum. Washed it all down with a big frosty mug of German beer. Still remember that fun tasty stuff. (And no, I do not drink warm beer, hahaha.) Gustav's! The German place there on the triangular corner where I used to eat was called Gustav's, now I remember.

After I ate... burp, ... I headed on into Wenatchee to see some folks there. Big strike out. My how things had changed in just 2 to 3 years? Scott and Bonnie had split up and moved. Reed was gone from his place, his neighbor said he moved to Spokane. Kenny and Darlene had reportedly moved off to Idaho. Got no idea whatever happened to Ghost Rider Taz, either. All my Wenatchee pals were missing. Shit dang, I didn't even get to see Officer Truman Douglas.

So next I'm gonna head over Blewett Pass and see if there's anybody in Ellensburg that I can still find.

Part 56: The California Rat Years

Headed Over Blewett to Ellensburg

I caught the old familiar Highway 97 going over the top of Blewett Pass, probably a 1 & 1/2-to-2-hour drive. I couldn't even begin to count the number of times I made this ride on the 74 AMF Chop, and it remains one of my favorite roads to ride, to this very day.

There was nice countryside where ever I looked. Mountains, rivers, trees, that's it. Hawks and eagles flying up high over the trees, wingtips spread out nice and wide, just soarin' and lookin' for some unfortunate little critter to swoop down upon and grab with them razor sharp talons, then rip the flesh to pieces with their wicked murderous hooked beaks and gobble up them guts. Oh my. Ain't nature sweet?

This tricky photo here is the 63 Vette with the sign announcing that you are headed up over Blewett Pass on the old highway. This road here is not Highway 97, it shoots off 97 and is allegedly the old route the stagecoaches used to take. There are many sharp twists and turns, dangerous cliffs with no guard rails, up and down turf. In other words, it's a really fun scenic ride, if you ain't in a big hurry.

Part 57: The California Rat Years

Where is Everybody?

Well, the ol' 63 Sting Ray made the rugged mountain stagecoach route just fine. Them 340 horses in the solid lifter 327 were workin' just fine on the big hills going up and down shifted good comin' downhill.

And while this car still had the old drum brakes,...which I adore,...they were also power brakes and were working just fine. It's kinda nice to have good brakes when you are running downhill in the mountains headed to a sharp dangerous bend in the switchback road with no guard rail with all them jagged rocks hunnerds of feet down below, hahaha.

When I got into Ellensburg, I went by Dane & Stacey's place, but nobody was there. I went by Chuck & Jodi's place but it looked like they had moved. Hmm. And I ain't got nobody's phone number with me and there weren't no cell phones back then.

So now what the fuck do I do? Hmm,...again. I did a puff. Then I drove over to my old flat I had on Water Street back in 1980. This was the flat where I used to park the 74 AMF Chopper inside back when it was still a beautiful show quality bike. And now I was hon-gry and Rossow's Burgers was still just acrost the street, so for old time's sake, I got me a tasty Campus Burger Basket and nice Chocolate Shake. Burp.

Then I pulled the 63 up into my old gravel parking spot in back of the flat and took this photo right where the 75 White Vette had its photo taken back in the fall of 1980, five years earlier. My how time flies. Then it was time to get ready to make the 2 day road trip back home to Cali-forn-y.

Part 58: The California Rat Years

Headed Back to San Francisco

Going back home I kinda wimped out on the fun but time-consumin' Highway 1 and 101, so I took the old familiar I-5 cuz I had spent a little bit longer in Washington than I had planned. So I made some good time cruisin' down the Interstate through Oregon down to the southern part of the state where I got a motel room for the night. No more camping now.

The next day was the familiar route drivin' by Mount Shasta on I-5 headed on into the Bay Area. I had been over this route so much I kinda felt like I knew which dogs lived at which houses and which farmer had gotten a new tractor, hahaha.

Anyways, once I got back, all the fun road trips were over for a little while, cuz winter was on its way, and although winters usually ain't all that bad in the Bay Area, they can still be very rainy and very windy. And while that brings us to the end of the 63 Sting Ray Road Trip, the rest of the saga continues. This photo is back home in San Francisco, out on the ocean. Can ya tell? I thought so, wink, wink.

Part 59: The California Rat Years

Christmas 1985

The mostly happy year of 1985 closed out with us still doing semi-OK up in the little Penthouse apartment. The 74 AMF was still rattin' out, but the 63 Sting Ray was doing a little better. Still no interior. The job fronts were doing OK for both of us.

This is what all our wonderful furniture looked like in that unit and yes, that wooden box coffee table is what I built choppers on, so now it's also a coffee table or beer holder, your choice.

For Christmas this year, Santy Clause brought me that nice Les Paul guitar. And just like most of the nice things I've got to temporarily enjoy in life, it also got ripped off a few years later. We got two of those white chairs at a furniture store, and that was the first new furniture either one of us ever had, cuz we always got used furniture.

But the real star of this photo is that wooden box coffee/beer table. Yep. Watch for future photos of that thing, cuz that is the wooden box the 74 AMF Easyriders Magazine Chopper gets built on in Seattle. And yes, I still have it and that brings us to the end of 1985 in the Haight. Whew.

Part 60: The California Rat Years

Rollin' Into Early 1986

This old photo here is from when Frisco Choppers was still down on Valencia Street..."Still in the Ghetto" as it said on the backs of their T Shirts. And "Across the Street from the Beautiful Valencia Gardens" was also advertised on their post cards and other funny stuff they sold. The Beautiful Valencia Gardens was the ghetto housing projects on the other side of Valencia.

Inside this shop they had some funny signs on the wall behind the counter. I wish I'da taken some pictures inside, but ya know how some folks are kinda itchy with cameras around, so I never pushed it. Anyhow, one of their funny signs said "Thank You For Pot Smoking" and the other one said "In God We Trust,...All Others Must Pay Cash". And that's the way it was back then, no fuckin' credit cards allowed.

As for their shop actually bein' in the ghetto? Now I ain't a-gonna say it was extra dangerous ridin' down there to it, cuz I never got stabbed, shot, or kilt myself, so I'll just say it was an "interestin' neighborhood" and let it go at that. This was back when Dennis and LA Gary ran the shop's parts counter and the other guys like Big Frank were in the back of the shop workin' on the mechanical end of things. And since there ain't no beautiful choppers in this photo parked out front like there normally was, I'm guessing this picture mighta been taken on a Sunday?

Now,...as to who took it? If the rear foot pegs were down, I'd say the Better Half jumped off quick in the middle of the street and took it, and if the rear foot pegs were up, I'd say either Oakland Steve or Dave with the 67 were sittin' on their Shovels in the middle of the street and took it. It is definitely taken from the middle of the street where the cars and city buses roam. But since I can't tell what the rear pegs are doing, and since it was 36 years ago, I'm drawin' a blank right now. Anyhow, I'll just say whoever took it took a chance of gettin' kilt and it's an old photo of an old chopper shop that don't exist anymore and an old photo of the old 74 AMF Chopper which does still exist today,...sorta,...but in a different version. How's that for a wrap-up?

Part 61: The California Rat Years

74 AMF Rat Chopper Frame

Here's a fairly close up shot of how shitty the front section of the 74 Rat Chop was lookin' at this stage of its life, hahaha. Geeze Louise. After all that hard work molding the frame, sanding the Bondo til my fingertips were split and bleedin', primin' it, sandin' it some more, then having my buddy Terry shootin' the Black Imron paint until it looked like a black glass Christmas ornament...and now just look at it. Yikes.

All that previous hard work, including the nice red pinstripes added in January of 1982, and then suddenly it was all broken, busted up out on the road at the end of February 1983 outside Portland Oregon. 13

months it lasted. That ain't much time to enjoy the fruits of your labor, is it? And here we've also got a good look at the San Francisco Blacksmith Shop's gusset, right behind where the Oregon logging truck stop guy welded the left side downtube back together. That front section of the frame is kinda ugly lookin' but that big ass gusset worked and held everything together for a few more years. It lasted until the summer of 1988.

And let's not forget that underneath that Paughco Mustang tank sits a 3 inch chunk of welded pipe which is holding the backbone of the frame together, See there? Now in the past, a lot of folks have said "hey man, that bike don't look too bad, why do you call it a rat bike"? The deal is they have no idea what is hidden from view, they don't know there is a welded pipe creature that lurks down below that gas tank.

And them steel bars in this picture mean this is once again taken at Roosevelt Tamale Parlor in the Mission, which was probably our main eatery back then. Now I'm gonna throw in another glorious old photo of the neck of the frame when it was still nice so's you can get the total "Before & After" effect thing.

Part 62: The California Rat Years

Top of Twin Peaks 1986

Here's a picture that can't be duplicated today. Why? Cuz they poured concrete parking lots and retaining walls all around the top of Twin Peaks and turned it into a fuckin' tourist stop for tour buses...groan.

This was Twin Peaks back in 1986 when it was the biggest ol' hill in San Francisco with nuthin' on top except wind and weeds, both kinds of weeds. The kind that grew outta the ground up there and the kind I had in me pocket. I'd ride up here at night...or during the daytime....and fire 'em up.

This shot is standing on top of the hill facing eastward over toward Oakland. And that big strip of lights ain't no airport runway, it's Market Street, the main drag in Frisco. That's Oakland over on the other side in the dark, and that little strip of lights going acrost the water is the Oakland Bay Bridge. None of it looks like this today.

Part 63: The California Rat Years

Night Time View out our Window

This is what it looked like at night time in the Haight up on top of our hill. Moon shinin' overhead and reflectin' off the Pacific Ocean. The dark spots in between the lighted spots are Golden Gate Park, where the Dead and other bands used to play.

Part 64: The California Rat Years

Time for Some Fun Again

Ya keep being a good little boy, payin' the bills on time, workin' the steady job, just hittin' little runs going on around the Bay Area, and next thing ya know, a coupla more months just drifted by and now it's once again time for the ultimate, the Redwood Run.

Here's 31 year old me now, ready to go down and kick the 74 AMF Rat over to head out to Garberville. It's already packed up with the tent and sleeping bag down in the garage. This is my light weight black leather jacket I got from Sears, Roebuck & Company back in 1975 for $99.99 and I got on my Frisco Choppers headband, shades in my hand, 1977 Easyriders Nasty Feet boots on my nasty feet and I'm ready to ride out. So that means this is early Friday morning.

Time to ride the loud nasty Rat Chop through the Haight and head on over to the Golden Gate Bridge entrance where Dave and Kent & Lori are gonna be. We'll do them illegal puff things on them big fat joints, get the good buzz going and then the funny part is gonna be ridin' against all that fuckin' Bay Area traffic. Cuz all them cages are gonna be drivin' INTO the city to go to work and we're gonna be ridin' OUTTA the city to go have some fun at the outrageous Redwood Run.

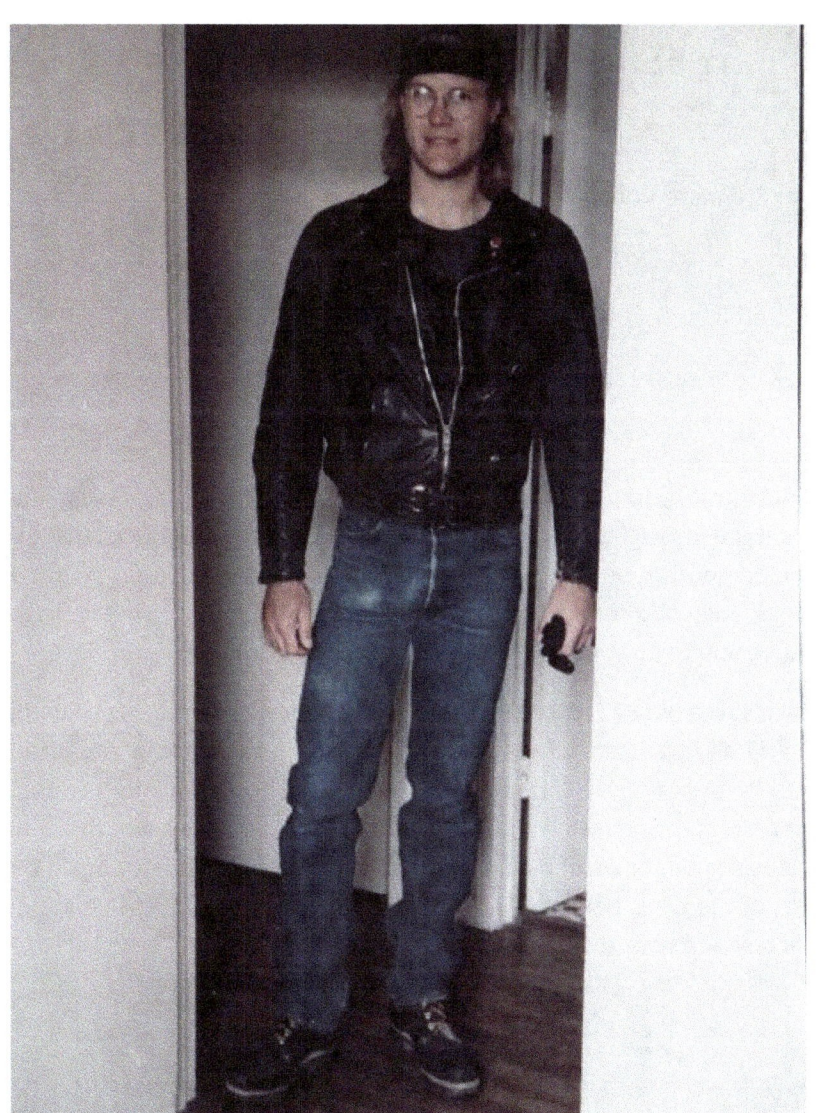

Part 65: The California Rat Years 1986

Redwood Run French's Camp

Our Standard Routine:

1. Ride chops to the front entrance of Golden Gate Bridge

2. Do big puffs on fat joints from Mendocino

3. Kick over the Shovelhead Choppers

4. Ride to the Redwood Run

Kinda basic routine to follow and it always seemed to work out just fine, We'd ride up Highway 101 for two hours or so, stop and stretch the legs and do another puff, munch on somethin' if ya feel like it, fill them gas tanks, then kick 'em over and ride the rest of the way. Next thing ya know, you're right here, at French's Camp in Garberville.

Dave's nice old 67 Shovel Chop aka Old Yellow always stands out in the crowd and it's usually the first thing I notice in these old photos from back then in the 1980s. My ol' 74 Black Rat Chop seems to be kinda embarrassed and is hidin' behind Dave's chopper. That's it with all the road gear campin' shit piled on the front end. I got no idea who all the rest of the bikes belong to. Maybe you might even see yours in here? That is,......if you're really old now, wink, wink.

Part 66: The California Rat Years 1986

Redwood Run "The Pit"

Here's a really sweet ol' Panhead Chopper, love this bike. It's set up just right in my humble opinion, and its stance is spot on. And his tent is made just like my green & yeller tent except for different colors. This is just a little part of the action in The Pit.

Your ticket price gets you one night of camping and a steak dinner on Saturday night, plus whatever band happens to be playing there. I forget which band played there this year, but it coulda been the Fryed Brothers Band outta Sacramento, (they actually ride) and then probably a bigger national name band after them. I got photos of the bands for the next 3 or 4 years still to come, but didn't get any this time, dang it.

Part 67: The California Rat Years 1986

Redwood Run "The Pit"

Here's some more Pit Action for ya. We got this fine ol' Red Knuckle here and the front end of Dave's 67 Old Yellow Shovelhead off to the side. That Knuckle is still packed, and its rider better get to settin' up his tent fast cuz the camp spots disappear right before your peepers at times.

That's why Dave and me started our Redwood Runs one day early, gettin' there to French's camp on Friday afternoon to pick the best spots. It cost us one night extra campin' fee, so what? At least we didn't get stuck with the last spots in the gawd damn gravel. Live and learn, my good buddy, live and learn.

Part 68: The California Rat Years 1986

Redwood Run & Duelin' Cameras

Check out this fine loooong stretched Shovel Chopper with that fantastic girder on it. I'm guessin' it's a Harmon? Stretched custom rigid frame, Sportster tank, Butt Bucket seats, kick start, mag wheels, man, this thing is right up my alley for 1970s Kool Chopper.

And then there's the guy in the background, bwahaha. Somewhere out there in California Motorsickle Photo World, he's got his photo of the left side of this chopper with me in the background taking my picture of the right side of the chopper with him in the background taking his picture of the left side of this chopper with me in the background taking my right side photo of this chopper with him in the background taking.....well, you get it. Right? We're kinda like a mirror image...maybe one of them tricky mirrors you see at the carnivals?

Part 69: The California Rat Years 1986

Redwood Run, a Blue One

After taking pictures of three Red Choppers in a row, my stoned self finally stumbled upon a Blue one! And a nice classic build it is, eh? Rigid frame, kick start, duck tail fender with the cat's eye tail light tucked inside, solo seat, fat bobs, shotguns, tool box, lots of shiny stuff around, and of course, that beautiful Panhead motor, all gussied up really nice.

Part 70: The California Rat Years

Redwood Run: Look! A River Rat

I realize I've blabbed a lot over the years about jumpin' in rivers. Whether the rivers were in Texas like the Guadalupe and Brazos, or up in Washington State like the Columbia and Icicle Rivers, or over yonder in California, like right here at the Redwood Run on the Eel River, I like to jump in 'em. I don't know why.

Maybe cuz I was born-ded in February which makes me an Aquarius water sign, or maybe it's because I get stinky and need to get clean, or maybe it's cuz I'm stoned and drunk and want something fun to do. I got no idea. All I know is I like to jump in rivers.

Sometimes the river water is kinda nice and not too cold, other times it's freezin' water that makes your hole pucker, sometimes it's just a nice refreshing river like this one where you can cool of from the hot overhead sun or do funny shit to help or hurt your hangover.

Sometimes I jump in with my clothes on, sometimes I strip down to my unmentionables, and sometimes I go skinny dippin', hahaha. Just depends on what mood strikes me. I guess I'm just a water rat. I'm almost positive this had to be a "Sunday Mornin' Comin' Down" type of river rat time. Cuz when was I ever not hungover at a Redwood Run on Sunday mornin'? Answer: Never.

And the river is the main reason I liked to pick out the first camp spots, cuz I'd get one right up next to it. When I'd get done baptisin' myself and come splashin' back up outta the water, I didn't have far to go to collapse by the 74 AMF Chopper and start in tokin' and drinkin' all over again. Party on!

Part 71: The California Rat Years

Redwood Run:

There's only one sad thing I ever discovered about the Redwood Runs. It's really sad when Sunday afternoon rolls around and ya gotta pack up your tent, shake the sand and dust outta yer sleepin' bag, roll 'em all up like a nice burrito and strap 'em to the chopper to leave,...sniff, sniff.

But before we'd kick our Shovel Chops over and shove off, we'd hang around just a little bit more, trying to soak it all in, cuz it would be another whole fuckin' year before we got to do it again. This fine Knucklehead just about sums up the entire run, if ya ask me. What a nice time capsule ride.

I wish to hell we could hop into a time machine and go back to these days and this wonderful place. But the photos and memory iz the only thing left. And it seems to me I can still remember smelling the exhaust fumes and maybe the aroma of some burnin' oil... just a little bit. You know what I mean, like some smoky exhausts kinda close to you? Maybe this fine old Knuckle here had a bit of that road worn smell when it fired up. Look at them pipes. I'll bet it does, what do you think, wink, wink? I'd like to sniff that Knuckle exhaust, just for old time's sake.

Part 72: The California Rat Years

Redwood Run: A Parting Shot

At the end of the Redwood Runs, Dave and me and Kent & Lori if they came along would go ridin' through the Big Giants before we headed back to civil-eye-zay-shun. I usually took pictures of them people and our bikes amongst the huge monstrous trees. But this time, maybe I was feelin' on the melancholy side? Who knows? I just looked straight up above us and took this one. Then we had a coupla puffs on some nice roaches we had left over, kicked the bikes to life and started our 4 hour ride back home,...so's we could all go back to work the next day.

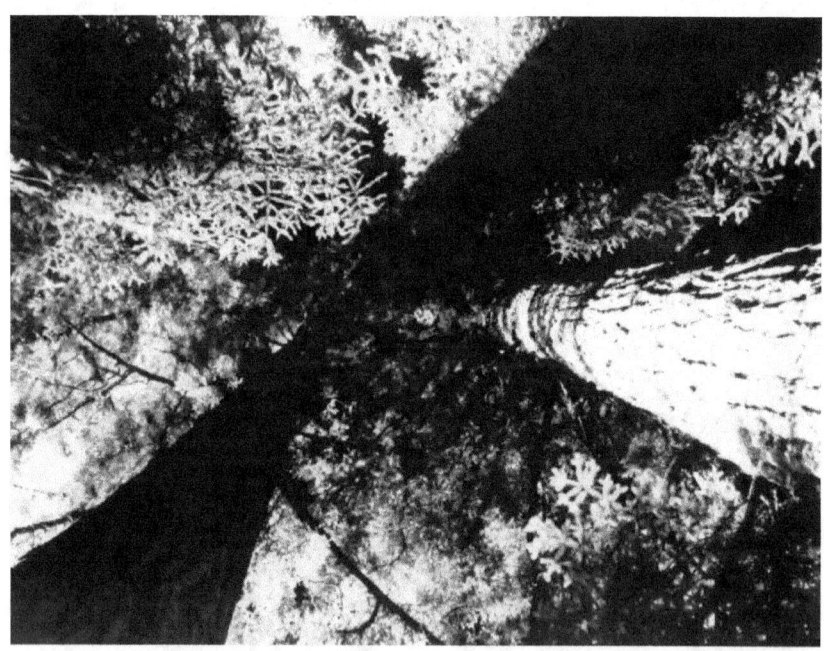

Part 73: The California Rat Years

End of Summer 1986

Only one thing stands out in my memory of the end of summer 1986. I had ridden the 74 Rat Chop over the big bridge and through the big tunnel to see Oakland Steve about some of his green stuff that needed a new home in my stash box. So I got the little baggie of green stuff from him,...we'll call it Oregano,......and I was headed back to the entrance to the Oakland Bay Bridge.

Everything was going normal, made that ride more times than I could count. Going up onto the bridge entrance, there is a winding circular entrance ramp, going slightly uphill and curving waaaaay to your right. It's a tight little loop where maybe you can do 25 or 30 mph if you're lucky and like leaning into curves really good,...like I do, hahaha. So I had the Rat Chop leaned over nice and low in the curve, chuggin' along in second, getting ready to hit the top of the ramp and shift into third, when it happened.

That back wheel slid out from under me like it was on ice! Instantly, I was down on the ground, slidin' along right behind and with the Rat Chop, kinda half on it and half off, if ya know what I mean? What the fuck was going on? Why am I on the ground sliding instead of going to the bridge? As I slid along the pavement getting some road rash on my right arm, I saw the Rat Chop bang into the curb and it jerked really big and the engine shut off.

I looked around me and the pavement was covered in oil. Great. Then this pedestrian guy comes runnin' up from outta nowhere, like he musta seen the whole thing from 50 feet away or so, cuz he was on the other side of the entrance ramp. He asked if I was OK? I said I guess. I'm standing up the Rat Chop while cars are going by me and I asked him what the fuck is all this oil doing on the ground? He told me about half an hour earlier, a VW Bug had blown its motor there and they had just hauled it away with a tow truck a few minutes before I got there.

Oh great. Well I guess that at least 'splains why I was slidin' on the ground, eh?

As for the chopper? It acquired a few more dings and scratches on it. But it's a Rat Chop, so who gives a rat's ass anyhow, right? I mean,... besides me? I kicked it over and rode on acrost the Bay Bridge back to the Haight. I parked the Rat Chop in its usual Rat Chop Spot and went upstairs to the little apartment on top of the hill. I pulled out Oakland Steve's Oregano and had me some. Well, maybe I had me a lot. And this picture here is what it looked like out our living room window around sunset time.

Part 74: The California Rat Years

Fall of 1986

In the fall of 1986, I was ridin' the 74 Rat Chop to a really nice construction job near downtown San Francisco, doing the interior of the Dolby Sound Studios building. That was where they added the soundtracks to movies. We built a miniature Art Deco movie theater inside their pre-existing old building. This theater had about 54 seats, if I remember correctly, with an elevated room in the back for the movie projectors to be anchored in.

The theater floor was cut and separated from the rest of the building and new walls were built on both sides of the cut floor. Imagine cutting a square outta the top of your kitchen table. The square still stays there, but it is separated from the rest of the table...see?

Then we did two structural steel stud walls on both sides of the cuts, making double walls that did not touch each other. No screws were allowed to fasten the studs to the top and bottom tracks. Everything had to be fastened with rubber isolators to eliminate vibration of any type. The result was we created what was then dubbed the "Quietest Room in California."

Meanwhile, the 63 Sting Ray was lookin' like this. I could get three different looks with one car,...the top down convertible, the white rag top up, or the hard top look. All this work was done on the same old primered 1963 ex-drag race car from Irving Texas, that I got back in 1976. These three photos were taken in San Francisco in the fall of 19 hunnerd and 86, and the Sting Ray even has its front bumper on it.

Part 75: The California Rat Years

December 18, 1986

Back in 1986, Christmas day fell on a Thursday. The Saturday before Christmas was the 20th. So, in order to start this sordid part of the story, we're going back to December 18 which was the Thursday before Christmas.

After work that fateful day, we got out the 74 Rat Chop and rode it through the scummy part of downtown, through the Tenderloin and on down to Chinatown for some good eats. Rat Chops are the best way to get around San Francisco, cuz you can cut in between the cars lined up at red lights and you can ride up on the sidewalks to park your Hawg. I never got a ticket for any of this stuff. And ya might as well ride a bike everywhere ya go cuz there ain't no empty parking spots for cars anyhow, unless you wanna wait for the next person who is double parking to leave their double parked spot so's you can get it and double park, hah.

The joint we were ridin' to for eats was called The Original Hunan and it was down on Kearny Street, kinda close by the Transamerica Pyramid, but The Original Hunan has since been gone cuz later on it got whopped really good and collapsed in the 1989 Earthquake. Anyhow, back to this Thursday night for our good hot Chinese eats. They had this dish called Marty's Special and it was based on delicious smoked ham and was like eating fire. This place was very authentic Hunan Chinese and we'd usually be the only white folks eatin' in their and they only had chop sticks, no silverware.

The Marty's Special was soooo hot and soooo tasty that ya just kept shovelin' it in, and the fact that your mouth is on fire didn't even matter. If I tried to eat that stuff today, I'd keel over with a heart attack, I'm sure. Anyway, this was back when we liked hot Mexican and hot Chinese food. We fucked up the first few times we ate there cuz we got beer to go with the food, Chinese beer called Tsingtao. We sadly discovered that drinkin' beer on top of the hot peppers only made your mouth and stomach foam even more, like you suddenly became a volcano ready to blow up. So in later days we drank plum wine with the eats.

What does all this ramblin' have to do with the 74 Rat Chop or 63 Rat Vette? Well just hang on, I'm gettin' to that part. It was at this place and this very night eating this fire hot dinner that we decided we needed to take a little weekend break before Christmas came in a few days. We thought it might be nice to take the 63 Sting Ray out for a drive up around Napa and Sonama that coming Saturday, the 20th. We planned to get outta town nice and early before any traffic, drive the 50 miles or so up to Napa, and then we'd be there cruisin' around in the nice hilly countryside fulla vineyards in the early morning hours still, before it got busy. Sounds like a good plan, let's do it.

When the check came, I paid it and left the little gal a nice tip and then we got to openin' and eatin' them little fortune cookie things just before we left. I never paid any attention to those fortune things, but this one kinda caught my interest. I always left those little fortune papers on the table, but this one I stuck in my wallet. I still have it today. What did it say?

Here it is. Now while the Better Half seemed to like the "happy and financially better" part, I was strangely fixated on the "difficult test" part, cuz to tell ya the truth, I had just about had enough of the difficult test shit the past few years, being homeless and having the chopper frame break in half on me on Oregon and catch on fire in the desert in Needles California was enough difficult test for me at the present. Now here we go again with even more difficult test shit?

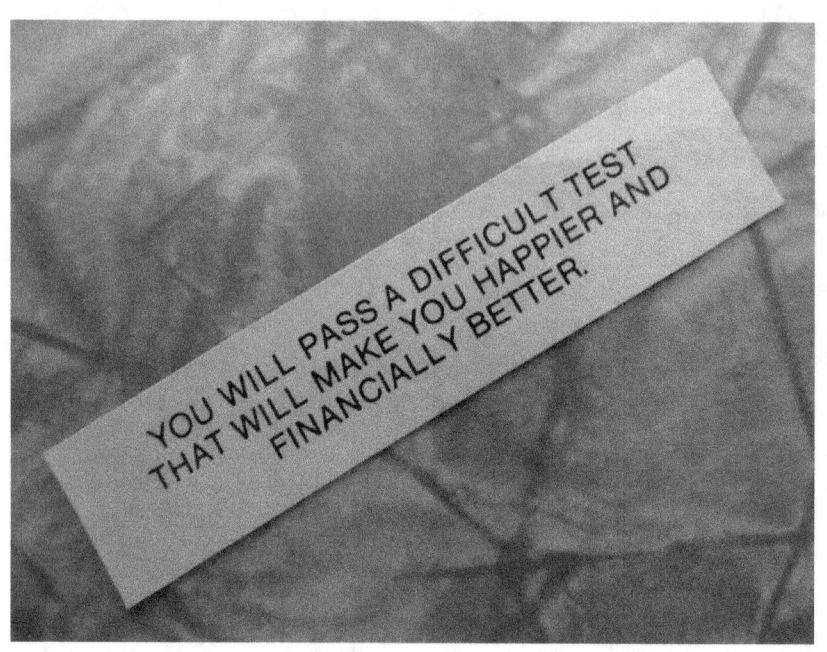

Part 76: The California Rat Years

December 19, 1986

Yay, it's Friday! And Friday means pay day, back when yer boss would actually give you a pay check that you could take to the bank and cash. Who remembers them days from long ago?

All day long at the job, I was itchin' to get off work, take that paycheck to the bank, then get back home and get the 63 Sting Ray gassed and cleaned up for our cruise up to Napa the next morning, which was to be our Saturday cruise day.

3:30 finally came, quittin' time, locked up the tools, said have a good weekend to the guys on the crew, went out to the sidewalk, bungeed my lunch box on the burned up back seat, kicked the Rat Chop over and rode off to the Wells Fargo Bank on up Market Street. After I was done inside the bank, I kicked the Rat over again and rode on back up the big 17th Street hill to the Haight and then rode on up even higher to our apartment building.

When I got there, I rode into the garage, parked the Chop back in my assigned corner spot, then I hopped into the Sting Ray and drove it down to the gas station on Oak Street. The fuel gauge still didn't work, hahaha, so I had to look down inside the tank to see how much gas I was gettin'. I filled that puppy up to the top where I could touch the gas. There, now it's good for all day long tomorrow.

I drove it back to the building, all excited about finally getting to take it out on a nice little road trip this time of year. Now our building had two different garage door openings, the one I used was on the left hand side which was the uphill side, while the one on the right hand side was for the lower level spots, cuz this was a two story parking garage, see? But there was also a single parking spot in the front, for the US Mail trucks to park, UPS guys, Fed Ex trucks, building maintenance guys, folks like that.

Those of us that lived in that big building and had cars would also park there to wash our cars,.....that is, if the water wasn't being rationed again, hahaha. So I pulled up into that empty parking spot, rolled up the windows, locked the doors, and I got out the water hose and sprayed down the Sting Ray good to get it soakin', see?

And then I went upstairs to our apartment and I got out my Bike & Car Washin' Bucket with the Turtle Wax car wash, the sponge, a coupla towels, two beers, and I went back down to wash the Sting Ray. Only problem was,..

.................................it ain't there. Some fuckin' asshole stole the 63. This is what was left for me to wash. Was this my "difficult test" from the fortune cookie the night before?

Part 77: The California Rat Years

December 19, 1986 It's Gone!

I stood there with my car wash bucket in one hand and a beer in the other, towel slung over my shoulder, in total shock and disbelief for a coupla seconds, thinking what the fuck happened. The 63 Sting Ray was gone! Some fucker or fuckers had stolen it. Fuck! Triple fuck!

I went back inside and rode the elevator upstairs and for the first time in my life, broke down and called the lame cops for help. Guess what? Them fuckers would not even send a squad car out to the scene of the crime. They said it was a 'victimless' crime. I said I certainly felt like a victim and stealing a car is still a crime, right? They said since nobody was shot, stabbed, or beat up, it was a victimless crime. First time in my life I ever heard that term. I knew I was gettin' nowhere fast with the fuckin' goon on the phone, so now it was time for me to make a personal visit to Pig Station.

I was fuckin' fumin' as I yanked on the 1975 AMF black leather jacket and went down to kick over the 74 Rat Chop. It fired right up and out the garage door we rode, right down the fuckin' hill to Pig Station. I rode down to the one called the fuckin' Park Police Station right off Stanyan Street, a few blocks down from where our old flat was.

I rode the loud nasty Black Rat Chop, with straight upsweep fishtail pipes and stroker motor, right up to their fuckin' front door, wracked off the pipes good and loud as my 'doorbell' to let them know I had just arrived, so now they got company. Then I shut it off, slammed the kick stand down and went stompin' in there mad as fuckin' hell. This is quite the switch, eh? Uusally they are the pissed off assholes coming after us nice motorsickle folks, but this time the shoe's on the other foot. I'm gonna show 'em what it's like to get yelled at by somebody that's really pissed off.

They kinda looked up in semi-surprise at wild and angry 6 foot 4 me in the black leather jacket and I think they instantly knew I was not there to give them free donuts or Girl Scout Cookies. I started in loud right off the bat to let them know where I fuckin' stood. I got nuthin' to hide. I was a tax payin' citizen that helped pay their fuckin' payckecks, I'd never been arrested in California, ain't even got one outstanding parking ticket and I ain't on probation, I am there to yell at them to help find the stolen 63 Sting Ray.

Next I had to show them ID,...which was actually current California ID this time, and I had to answer questions while this lady filled out the paperwork. She asked if I had car insurance, I said yes. Meanwhile, I am fumin', thinkin' the thieves are making an even cleaner getaway right now as the cops and me were bullshittin' about all this crap. After we got the paperwork done, I explained to them that this car wasn't a regular old 1963 used car I bought off a used car lot. I explained how I had about 10 years of my life in it doing the restoration work, and then I think maybe,...just maybe,...they started getting the idea how fucking pissed off I was. They said they'd keep an eye out for it. Great. That will help me sleep just fine tonight. Geeeze.

Next I went back outside, kicked the still warm chopper over again and took off back up the hill where our building was, and I started circling the neighborhood like a hungry buzzard looking for its next meal victim. My mind was rushin' 190 mph. Two things popped up. Maybe some punk ass kids took it for a joy ride, or else professional thieves got to it with a tow truck. I don't think I had been inside the apartment long enough for anyone to hot wire the car. Then my mind flashed back to maybe 2 weeks earlier.

There had been three gangly teenage snot nosed brats walking down the sidewalk while I was just pulling the Sting Ray into the driveway to go in the garage. One of them had said "Nice car" while another one of them said "How much would you sell it for?" I told them thanks and said it wasn't for sale. Then one of them sez the tired old standard line 'everything is for sale for the right price.' I had said "Not this car. It ain't for sale, period." Then one of them had smarted off, "Then we'll steal it" and the other two laughed.

I hadn't paid any attention to them when they said that, but now I suddenly did. I started out on the top of the hill where our driveway was, in the exact spot where the thieves stole the 63. It is a very high hill, one of the highest in the city and a car can roll for blocks and blocks going down hill there. So now I'm lookin' down the hills and streets, wonderin' which way they mighta gone, if they were doing a joy ride in it. Since the 63 had Poweer Steering, that meant it would be extra difficult to steer without the engine running, right? So I'm ridin' down the hills with the straightest and easiest direction to drive a car with stiff steering. Nuthin' turned up. Didn't see shit.

I rode around the neighborhood til it was dark, then gave up for the night. The next morning I started out all over again. I viewed the streets of San Francisco's Haight Ashbury district as a giant waffle. First, I rode up and down all the streets going north and south, and I did that from Stanyan Street all the way down to Divisidero. Nothin' turned up. I had my eyes peeled for any glint of silver blue paint or a chrome bumper sticking out of a garage or from behind a bush,... anything,... anywhere. Nuthin' again.

Next I did the same thing on the chopper, but this time I covered all the streets running east and west parallel with Oak and Page. Still nuthin'. I began thinking maybe some pros got it with a tow truck after all. I figgered if kids had gotten it, they woulda ridden it off somewhere until it crashed, then jumped out and ran. The 63 was nowhere to be seen anywhere in that neighborhood, it was either gone or hidden really good.

I called up my ridin' buddy Dave with the Chopped 67 Shovel Old Yellow and told him what was up, just in case I didn't make it in to work Monday morning, cuz him and me were working on that same Dolby Sound Studios job together. I spent Sunday out ridin' on the Rat Chop, widening my search for my beloved, and now missing, Silver Blue 63

Sting Ray. Never saw one damn clue of anything. While I had been at the cop shop, I had given them my home phone number and the jobsite number to call, just in case they ever found anything.

I spent Saturday night and Sunday night with no sleep. Monday morning came and I rode the Rat Chop back in to work. Our superintendent there was a nice guy named Rich and his foreman was a car guy named Ray, and he had an old Cord himself, with those cool hide-a-way head lights that he had done a frame off restoration on a few years earlier. So Ray was the main guy there at the job that felt my pain.

So I set in to work that Monday morning with no more 63 Sting Ray. Luckily I didn't fuck anything up at work and didn't cut off any fingers, hardy har har. There ain't no picture to go with this moanin' drivel cuz I ain't found the car yet to take a picture of. Fuck!

Part 78: The California Rat Years

December 22, 1986 Monday

And just like that,...in the quick wink of a bloodshot eyeball on that fateful Friday evening, we went from being a One Car & One Bike Family down to a No Car & One Bike Family. Monday morning I begrudgingly rode the Rat Chop in to work. Maybe working will take my mind off the Sting Ray being stolen? Yeah, right, who the fuck am I tryin' to kid? My own damn self?

So the Monday work day is draggin' on, an hour seemed to take a week. All I could think about was all the work that had gone into that 63 over the past 10 years, starting back in 1976 in Dallas, and it's now stolen. My work and ridin' buddy Dave kept tryin' to cheer me up, talking about our Shovelhead Choppers and shit, but I guess I was kind of a wet blanket at that time.

Then around 2:00 after lunch break, Ray the foreman comes up to me and sez "Dave, there's a phone call for you and it's the cops." Now normally that would be bad news, right, hahaha? But I was glad to hear from 'em. The cop guy on the phone said they had found the car and it was in the impound lot right that instant. Yay!

They got the Sting Ray back, now I was happy as a pig in slop. I asked the cop guy if I could come down and get it right now.   He said something like "According to this report right here, it is not in driving condition." I asked if the fuckin' thieves wrecked it. He said "Did this car have any damage on it when it was stolen?" I said "No, it has a brand new 3200 dollar paint job on it from Rick Brown's Corvette Corner shop over on Harrison."

The cop is still reading his report and sez "Well now it's got front end damage and looks like they took the motor out." Oh great, just fuckin' great. So they stole it to get the motor? And then wrecked it either before or after the motor got yanked? So I started thinking about what

I was gonna do to get the car up and running again and I told the boss man I needed to take off the rest of the afternoon and Ray said sure, go for it, no problem. I didn't even bother to change my work clothes. I've got on my Redwing boots, white Ben Davis carpenter overalls and my black leather jacket ridin' on the chopper to go see the Sting Ray, hahaha. Musta been a sight.

Our job site was kinda close to San Francisco General Hospital. And the Hall of Justice, where I was riding to, was a few blocks over on Bryant Street, I think it was a 7 story building. I rode the Rat Chop over the few blocks and went up inside to meet with a guy named Inspector Peck, an older guy maybe in his late 50s,...about 10 years younger than I am today, hahaha. He told me to come with him and we'll go to the impound lot to see the Sting Ray. He said he'd gimme a ride over to the lot, but I told him I didn't wanna leave my bike there, cuz it might get umm,......STOLEN? And I wasn't joking, I was serious as shit. I ain't trustin' nobody at this stage of the game.

Inspector Peck said for me to follow him, so I did. Can ya imagine what that looked like? Wish I had a picture of that action. Me in white overalls and black leather jacket on a loud nasty black Rat Chop, getting a fuckin' Police Escort over to the impound lot, that seemed really funny to me at that moment, until we got there, anyhow. That impound lot was really strange, it was like a combination wrecking yard and towed cars, junk everywhere, wrecked cars, stolen cars, along with other fine cars like new Mercedes and Lincolns that had been towed in for whatever reasons.

We walked around one of the corners of cars and there it was! I nearly threw up. It looked like my old 63 Sting Ray pal had been murdered. No engine, my ass? Howzabout no nuthin' left? Them fuckin' asshole thieves had stripped the car with a jig saw and Skill saw. How do I know that? Cuz I'm a carpenter and know what those cuts look like. I could tell by the scratches in the paint where the bases of each different saw had run. They cut off the nose of the car to get the head lights, dropped a Skill saw down through the floor hump to get the tranny out from the top, it was pure murder. It seemed like there was more gone than there was left. I actually felt like I was gonna throw up when I saw it. It was sickening.

Well, next up on the agenda was to get the Sting Ray outta there and over to,......umm,...Rick's shop? I sure as hell couldn't take it back home. So I used their phone in the lot office and called up AAA Road Service, which I had joined back when I was sanding the body on the car and got stuck in the sand at Ocean Beach. And then I called up Rick to let him know I'd be bringing the Sting Ray back to his shop, so he'd better "Make Room for Daddy",...which was a Danny Thomas TV show fer you younger folks.

Once the AAA tow truck driver got there, he balked at towing the 63 to the shop. He said he was paid to tow drivable cars which had broken down. I told him this WAS a drivable car just 3 days ago and now I needed help to get it to the Corvette shop, so he finally hooked me up and got it going. I mean, cripes, it was only a few blocks away over on Harrison and 18th, so gimme a break and do your job like I do mine, OK?

As we got to the shop, the guy undid the Big Hook, and we pushed the Sting Ray's carcass into Rick's shop. You shoulda heard the groans and sighs from the crew there when they saw it. Nobody had any idea it had been ripped off and stripped. So now you can feast your peepers on what the fuckin' asshole thieves did to the 63 Sting Ray.

Part 79: The California Rat Years

December 23, 1986 Tuesday Morning

After the 63 Vette Carcass got towed in to Rick's shop, I called the job site and told the boss man I was taking off Tuesday and he understood why. Inspector Peck had told me the 63 carcass was found on the corner of Cortland & Prentiss Streets, still remember that location. That intersection is just south of Bernal Heights, east of Mission Street, down in The Barrio.

I grabbed my old 1930s Al Capone Gangster Overcoat outta the closet and grabbed my Fedora hat. Yes, that's right, I had a fuckin' Fedora hat, hahaha. I walked down to Haight Street and got one of them little tiny throw-away disposable cameras with a 12 shot roll of film in it. I hopped on the bus and headed off for The Mission Street bus and then on into the deep Barrio. It was kinda cold and clammy, so I was not overdressed, I sorta fit in with the elements.

The Mission Street bus let me off by Cortland and from there I had a 17 block walk uphill to get to Prentiss. Scummy area, shall we say? I got to the intersection where The Murder Victim had been disposed. I walked up to the house on the southwest corner of the intersection and knocked on the door. A rather rotund Hispanic fellow answered the door and he looked pissed that I was buggin' him. So in my politest/hidden anger voice I could muster, I asked him "Excuse me, don't mean to bug you. But do you remember the wreckage of a car that was left here on this corner?" Luckily, he spoke English cuz my Spanish ain't so hot, I can order in Mexican restaurants and that's about it.

The guy said "Yes! That wreck was there in front of my house for two days! I had to call the cops FOUR TIMES to get it hauled away!" He started to close the door, but I stuck my foot in a little bit and said "Just one more thing. Which way was it facing?" He said "That way!" and pointed to the north, then he slammed the door shut. OK, nice, now we're gettin' somewhere.

The back left corner of the 63 Carcass had white chalky paint on it, the kind of paint GM and Chevy used on their pick up truck bumpers back then, just like the white paint used on my dad's Chevy pick up. The sides of the 63 had some light tan colored paint scrapes on both sides. So Detective Me is lookin' for a garage with tan colored door jambs on it, where they pushed it in and out, and any vehicle with a white bumper that might have my silver blue paint on it from when they pushed the carcass away from where they had stripped it.

I knew it had to come from somewhere kinda nearby, cuz even as stupid and lazy as most fuckin' thieves are, most of them are smart enough to not dump the evidence right in front of their own place, right? Yet they still had to get rid of the carcass and with the condition it was in, they could not have gone far with it. So, I pulled the big Chicago gangster coat collar up as high as I could and pulled the hat down low, trying to hide as much white skin and blonde hair as I possibly could. Now it's time to go to work and find the fuckers that did it.

Now that I knew the 63 carcass was facing to the north, I started walking up yet another hill, headed south, lookin' for any type of evidence. When I got up to the top of that hill, I could not fuckin' believe what I was seeing. Guys were stripping cars right there on the street in broad daylight. They had fairly new Chevys, Fords, Buicks, Oldsmobiles, Pontiacs, you name it, mostly American made cars, sitting up on jack stands yanking off wheels, taking out interiors, pullin' out motors, you name it. There was so much action going on, wrenches were tingling up and down the street like wind chimes. So I leaned up against a tree and took a photo of all that action, showing proof of the cars being stripped on both sides of the street, right out in the open, not even trying to hide what they were doing. They didn't seem to have a worry in the world.

Then I moseyed on along the sidewalk some more. I stayed up close to the buildings in the shadows, trying to not attract any attention to myself. And then, there they were. A roofing crew. 6 guys working on a flat roof. They had a work truck there and it was a combination of GM and Chevy parts and emblems, with different colored hood and doors, …. busted. In other words, a stolen truck put together with parts form other stolen trucks? And they had Skill saws and jig saws with them, both on the ground and up on the roof with them.

I could hear the Skill saw up on the roof running at that very moment, cuz I am a carpenter after all and know what the hell a Skill saw sounds like. There were chunks of 2 X 4s and pieces of plywood layin' on the ground and sidewalk. And now I'm getting really pissed, cuz I am 99.9% sure I am looking at the guys that stole the 63 Sting Ray and I'm watching them work with the very tools they stripped the 63 with.

So, I took some more pictures. Then I got up close to the GM/Chevy hybrid truck and there it was! My fuckin' silver blue paint on the driver's side of the front bumper. This is the truck they used to push the carcass away with. Has to be, cuz there's my paint, dammit. Took another picture of that evidence.

Then I kept walking and found the tow truck they probably used when they stole the 63. A red and white flat bed tow truck, kinda beat up, and it said "Jay's Towing" on the driver's door and "J&J Towing" on the passenger door. No license tag at all on the front, and one that said "USA #1" on the back. Took pictures of that tow truck, front and back, both sides. I took pictures of the guys up on the roof. Granted, I couldn't get close up enough to show their stupid mugs, but you get one or two of them busted, they'll squeal on the rest. "There is no honor among thieves."

So with the little camera all loaded up now with its 12 shots of evidence, I thought I now had a slam dunk case against the asshole thieves. I hoofed it back down the 17 blocks, walkin' back to Mission and caught the bus. That Mission bus took me back to Market Street where I hopped off and caught the #7 Haight Street bus. It took me almost all the way back home, but I jumped off first at one of those "Overnight/One Hour Film Developing" places. I went inside and flipped the guy at the counter a 20 dollar bill.

I told him although this is a cheap-ass little throw away camera, it has some VERY important photos inside it and they were gonna be used as evidence in a criminal car theft case. I asked him to purdy please do them next. Told him I lived just up the hill and I'd be back in 10 mintues for them, and then I'll be taking them down to the Hall of Justice on Bryant Street. The guy said OK. I walked up the big ass hill on Buena Vista,......getting in a lot of hill climbing this day,......and I went up inside the apartment, yanked off my under cover photographer disguise clothes, put on my regular chopper clothes, went back down to the garage, kicked over the 74 Rat Chop and rode it back down to Haight Street and got the photos.

OK, now I'm ridin' off to the Hall of Justice to see that Inspector Peck, the guy in the Auto Theft Department who was assigned to handle my case. Here's another picture of what they did to the 63. I guess I no longer hafta worry about the gauges not working, eh?

Part 80: The California Rat Years

December 23, 1986 Tuesday Afternoon

After I switched clothes and hopped on the Rat Chop and got the evidence photos from the film developing shop on Haight Street, I rode on over to Bryant Street to the Hall of Justice Building. I locked up the chopper outside and went up to the 6th Floor to the Auto Theft Division offices. Then I walked into Inspector Peck's office, kinda unannounced, but after all, I was on official business, right?

Nobody else was in his office this afternoon, just him, so I plopped myself down in the chair in front of his desk, and I guess I was kinda smilin' for the first time in four days. I reached into my jacket pocket and pulled out the dozen evidence photos. I fanned them out on his desk right in front of him like a deck of fresh poker cards.

As I slid each picture over in front of him, I explained what each one was. It went like this, "Inspector Peck, here is the area at Cortland and Prentiss Streets where they stripped and dumped off my Sting Ray. Here are the guys up on the roof that probably did it. Here are the tools they used to strip my car. Here is the hybrid truck they used to push my Vette's chassis away with, and as you can see, there is my silver blue paint on it. Here is the fake ass illegal unlicensed tow truck they are using to steal cars in broad daylight. And here they are stripping cars right out in the open."

Now I guess I expected the flatfoot to at least be semi-excited that I was helping him do his job,.....for free, I might add. You might think he'd reach over and grab his phone and call one of his cop buddies and say some shit like 'hey, we got a guy here with evidence on that car theft ring we've been looking for.' But no. None of that happened. Cuz the Cop World is not the Real World. The Cop World doesn't give a shit what happens to those of us that pay their salaries. This is what happened in the Cop World that day.

Inspector Peck: "This is all circumstantial evidence and you've got no business being out there doing this. You are going to get yourself hurt or maybe even killed."

Me: "I want the fuckers that stole my 63 to go to prison and I am gonna do everything that I can to help you put them fuckers in the San Quintin State Pen."

Peck: "You've got insurance, don't you?"

Me: "Yes, of course, but that's not the point. What you fail to understand is I have 10 years of my life tied up in this car. It means waaay more to me than your car does to you."

Peck: "This is official police work and you have no business getting involved with it."

Me: "It's MY car that was stolen and stripped and that gives me the right to get VERY involved with it. Are you nuts?"

So it went back and forth like that, without the cop ever giving two shits for what had happened. I got pissed off even more, he cared less even more, like I was boring him. I finally realized I was gonna get nowhere with this ignorant uncaring tax payer funded clod. I went from being semi-happy back to being a pissed off fucker again, just like that.

I got up out of his chair, and as I got ready to leave his office for the final time and never come back, I said "Oh,.....and Merry Fuckin' Christmas,...........ya lazy prick." Then I stood there and stared at him with the Steelie Eyed Chopper Rider Stare for about 3 seconds in case he wanted to say anything else. He did not. He just sat there and stared at me like the piece of pig turd that he was. My final words to him as I shut his door were "Why don't you change the name of this building to the Hall of Injustice, since that name fits you better?" Never saw the fuckin' Peck Prick again.

Next I rode the Rat Chop back over to Rick's Corvette shop on Harrison and told him all that had happened. Rick rolled his eyes and said "Just be glad you've got insurance. Think how you'd feel if ya didn't have it." Then Rick said the next step in this ordeal would be dealing with the insurance company. He told me to ask them if I could buy the wreckage back from them after they settled. I asked him why? He said "Offer them two grand for it, then I'll give you the two grand and you'll be even and they can cash you the rest of the way out. You'll have cash and be free to go find another Mid-Year again."

I said OK, and I was kinda using Rick as my father figure cuz he had dealt with this type of stolen car shit many times, while it was my first time. So the Dead 63 Sting Ray Carcass had a new home at Rick's shop.

Part 81: The California Rat Years

December 24, 1986 Christmas Eve

Christmas Eve was Wednesday, not a holiday for us construction workers, so I went in to work with the rest of the crew,......finally. My guts were churnin', my punkin' head was still spinnin', but I guess the worst part was over now? At least the 63 wasn't just "missing" forever. I got to see what was left of my beloved Sting Ray, they call that "closure" these days, and I found the culprits myself, but did not shoot them, so I was still outta jail. Who knows, maybe some half-decent cop might get a whiff of the foot work I had done to collect the evidence for them and be on the case? Or maybe not? We'll see.

So that's how I spent Christmas 1986.

Going into the New Year, January of 1987, I did the salvage & wreckage buy-out from the insurance company as Rick had suggested. Then he cashed me out for what I had given them, which was 2,000 clams. The last thing for me to do was sign over the 63 Sting Ray's title to Rick,...sniff, sniff. It's sad even now, thinking about this day these 35 years later. It still hurts.

All those 10 years, since 1976, working on that crazy old car, my dad working on it, taking it from the burned out old drag race car into something that was almost beautiful. Now it's all gone.

Oh! And one more thing about this day. Rick comes up to me, points over to the corner of his shop where some cardboard boxes are and sez "Your Al Knoch interior came in today."

Shit dang! In all the excitement, I had totally forgotten about that. A few days before it got ripped off, I had ordered a new Al Knoch interior set, two new seat foams, new black vinyl seat covers, black vinyl center arm rest, black carpet for the front and back sections of the car, plus two black vinyl door panels. That was the factory correct colored interior and it was all top notch quality stuff, exact reproductions. I got

THAT close to having the car totally restored. I asked Rick what to do with it now? He said he'd keep the Al Knoch stuff and eventually rebuild the car. But it was gonna take a while,...a loooong while as it turned out.

Meanwhile, I'm waiting for the insurance company to cash me out and Rick already had a used although damaged 1963 hood for the Sting Ray. And that's the title sitting on the hood that I had just signed over to him.

Part 82: The California Rat Years

January 1987: Movin' On Along

So there was some tricky legal mumbo jumbo crap about what we had to do with the 63 Corvette salvage, and here's the wringer they ran me through. The insurance dude and me haggled back and forth about what we thought the car was worth. (Lookin' back, I shoulda haggled harder and longer.) We settled at 18,000 even. I thought that was purdy good, cuz I figgered I had just under 12,000 bucks in it, and they say ya ain't supposed to count your own labor hours,...for some reason, hmm.

So at first I thought I was makin' out kinda OK. And in hindsight, I was lucky the thieves left the carcass on the street to be found purdy quick. In a case where your car is stolen and they do not find it for a while, there is a longer waiting period before they can declare it officially stolen and gone,...like 30 days or 60 days. So finding it on the street, as maddening as it was, helped me outta this mess in the longrun. So 18,000 is what the deal was to settle.

But I had $500 deductible, so that cut their payout to me down to 17,500, still kinda OK with me. I signed the title over to them, they gave me the check. Then Rick wanted me to buy the salvage back, cuz the owner of the vehicle does have that choice, so I gave the insurance dude 2,000 back for the title and now I am the official owner of the title and the pile of engine-less fiberglass for a coupla hours or so. Then Rick gave me the 2,000 back and I signed the title over to him, so now it's his heap of fiberglass carcass. Now I am walking away free of the entire stolen car mess and I got 17,500 to go look for another Sting Ray. Yay. So that left Rick with a 63 Convertible carcass and a title he got for only 2,000 bucks, I walked away with 17,500, and the insurance company got a 17,500 business tax write off for their effort.

After work and on the weekend, I'd head out on the chopper for the East Bay cuz they had more used car lots for muscle cars over on that side. Yikes. What few Sting Rays there were,...they were already asking 22,000 to 24,000 for them, and even more. Gulp. And this was 1987. I was beginning to worry that I had suddenly been priced out of the market and could no longer afford a car like I had paid cash for 10 years earlier.

I even thought about going back with the 63, but it woulda cost me waaaay more than it was worth to rebuild it, and how long would it take on my meager carpenter pay? Rick could do it, cuz he owned the shop and could have his own guys work on it in between their regular customers' jobs and do it at his cost. So I felt like I was getting boxed in. Then I picked up the newest issue of Vette Vues Magazine and found this ad that caught my bleary eyeballs.

This is the page I saved from back then and it's the ad I drew the box around. "1964 Convertible, 2 tops, 327/300 HP, air, PS, PB, PW, backup lights, excellent White paint, new Black interior, everything works, numbers match, $15,500. Call Ken,..."...so I did.

The first thing Ken told me over the phone was the ad was supposed to say "like" new Black interior, he said it was still the original interior and was in really nice shape, like new. That is even better to me. He also said it had just over 30,000 miles on it. Only bad thing was he is in Indiana, not in the East Bay. And the other thing was, he did not mention in the ad whether it had a 4 speed or not, didya catch that one, wink, wink?

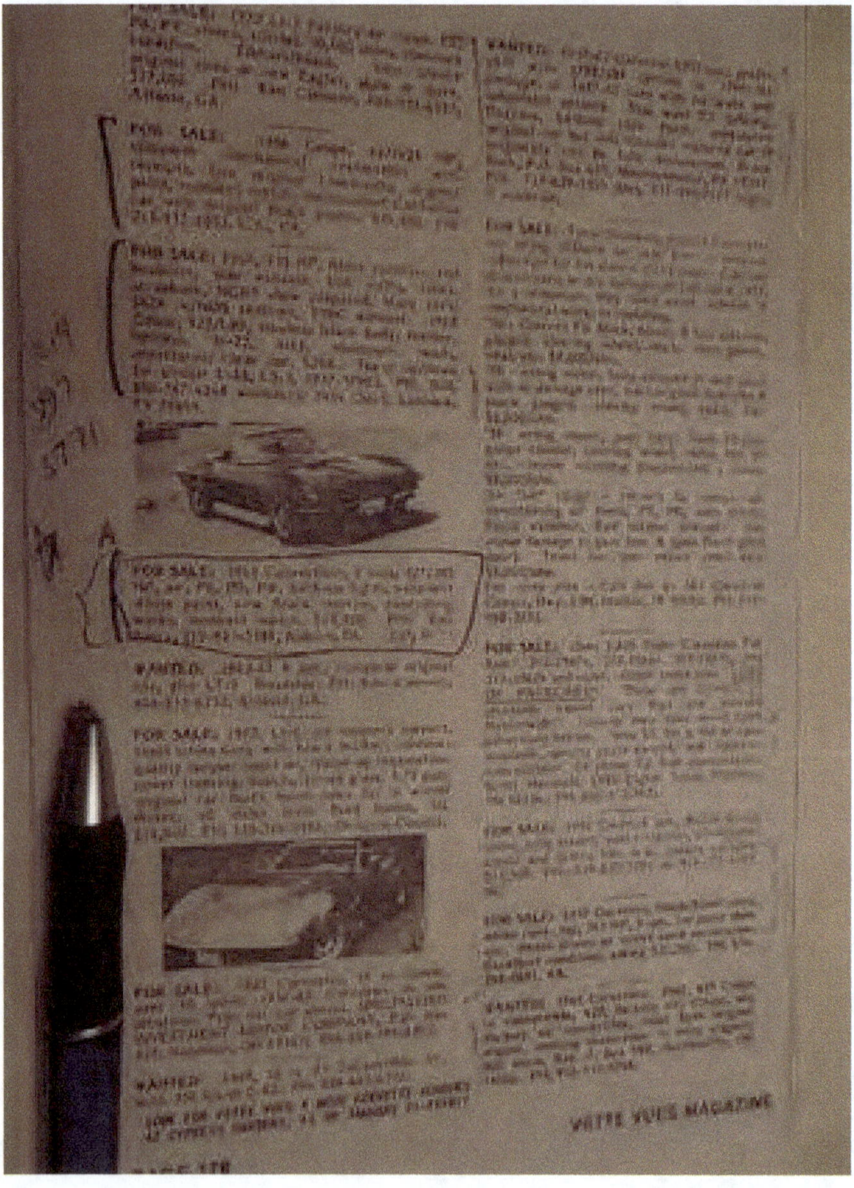

Part 83: The California Rat Years

A 1964 Convertible Sting Ray

After I called Ken with the 64 Convertible in Indiana, he said he'd send me a coupla photos of his White 64 for me to check out. They showed up in the mail a few days later and I was liking what I saw.

Actually, I loved everything about the 64 except for one little thing, and that thing wasn't so "little" to me at the time. Although the ad did not mention it, the car also had a "PG." That is Corvette Slang for a Power Glide transmission, or what some older guys called the Power Slide tranny, hahaha. It's a 2 speed automatic tranny. I wanted a 4 speed with a clutch to do burnouts with. But on the flip side, the car was loaded with every option you could get back then, except it did not have Fuel Injection and I didn't wanna mess with that mechanical Rochester injection set up anyhow. That is Rocket Science to my simple noggin.

The main draw on this car was it had Factory Air Conditioning, and it worked. 1964 was only the second year that option was available. Only 1,988 Corvettes had the AC option from the factory and most of those were the Coupes, so to find an air conditioned convertible was very rare. I was very interested.

I made plans to fly to Indiana to see this car. I had never done anything like that before in my entire life, but here I go. And I kinda had to cuz the California market had already priced me out. If I want another Sting Ray, I'd better act fast. Ken was in Auburn Indiana, and right acrost the border from him was a Vintage Corvette Dealer called Pro Team, and they claimed to have over 100 Vintage Corvettes inside their showroom, all pre-1973 models.

So if the White 64 doesn't work out for me, I can rent a car and drive to Ohio and get one there. Remember this was way before getting cars online. All we had were the old magazines and to go to the car lots in person. So I ain't got much of a choice in the matter. Here's the photos of the White 64 that Ken sent me.

Part 84: The California Rat Years

February 1987 Off Into the Wild Blue Yonder

I packed a few clothes in the Rat Chop road bag, then went down to the garage and grabbed the tool bag off the Rat Chop, brought it back up with me and stuck the tools in the road bag with the clothes. Then I rode the 74 Rat Chop over to the bank and cashed that check for 17,500. The next mornin' I took off in a big plane headed to Indiana. Plan A was,... after I was supposed to land in Indianapolis, I was supposed to catch a little puddle jumper plane to Auburn and Ken was supposed to meet me at the airport there.

At first I was feelin' really good about going there to get a 1964 Sting Ray for a lot less money than they cost-ted in California. Then I started thinkin' how I was gonna be drivin' a strange 23 year old car, one that I knew absolutely nothin' about, headed out cross country 2,300 miles all the way back to California,......in the middle of February winter time. Yikes. Am I totally nuts now? Had all this Stolen Corvette Drama finally burned out what little I had left of my brain? Maybe so, I dunno.

Also, I could not take a Cashier's Check with me, cuz I had no idea who it would be made out to, see? So I had me that big ol' wad of cash in my pocket, right next to my ultra sharp Puma knife. And then I started feelin' nervous about havin' that much cashola on me. Cuz Ken knew I was coming with the cash, and he was a total stranger to me.

For all I knew, he could be waitin' at the dinky little airport in Auburn with three good ol' boys, knock me in the haid, dump my carcass out in the creek somewhere in the deep woods, and nobody would ever know what happent to me,...right? Four of 'em could pocket a little over 4 grand each, I had already done the math to see how much they'd make knockin' me off.

Thoughts like that can run through my mind at times, especially when I'm by myself. This is what 17,500 looked liked. Most loot I ever had in my life. And I'm gonna blow it all on a strange old car and try to drive it cross country over 2,000 miles, hmm. Kinda crazy and excitin',..... eh?

Part 85: The California Rat Years

February 1987 Auburn Indiana

Transferred planes in Indianapolis from the big 'un jet airliner to the li'l puddle jumper single prop plane. Landed in Auburn Indiana and there was Ken to meet me at the airport. Didn't have a clue who to look for, but there weren't that many people there so it was kinda easy to figger out who was who.

I grabbed the duffel bag and we headed out the door of their little airport. I was wanting to go rent a car to drive around in and was gonna get a motel room. But Ken insisted he'd drive me around in his brand new Silverado pick 'em up truck and said him and his new wife had tons of room at their new house they had just built and I should stay there.

This made me feel uncomfortable. I said shit like "Ken, thanks for the offer, but I'm not 100% sure I am getting your car from you." He countered with "Once you see it, you'll get it." Kinda confident, eh? I told him that I needed to get a rent car cuz I wanted to drive over to Napoleon Ohio to look at the cars at Pro Team. Ken laughed and said "I know exactly what kind of cars Terry sells at his place. I will gladly drive you over there, it's just across the border anyhow." I said "I will feel very strange if I buy a car from Pro Team after taking advantage of your hospitality." Ken laughed again and said "If you don't want the 64, there's plenty of other people who WILL want it."

Well, OK, it's on. I will take him up on him being the Private Chauffeur and filling in for the Auburn Hotel for a night or two. He drove us through downtown Auburn, which was a really cool little town where they used to make the old Auburn cars back in the day. We went by the Auburn Cord Duesenberg Automobile Museum. Cords? Now my ol' Foreman Ray with the Cord is gonna like the fact I was in his Cord's hometown, hahaha.

We drove on out through the edge of town into the woods and finally came upon Ken's new house. I'll call it a beautiful mansion out in the woods, how's that? Ken and Kathy had a big swimmin' pool in the back, and the pool house they had was probably as big as our little house we live in today, so Ken is loaded?

First thing we did was go out to his extra 3 car garage on the side and took a look at the White 64, which was sitting next to his wife's Silver Blue 58. The 64 was nice,...very nice. Popped the hood, it was all there and looked to be original. I'd been in the NCRS since 1984 so I kinda knew what to look for, and this car had it all together. It actually was an unmolested Sting Ray. I crawled underneath it as far as I could and the frame was nice and solid, rust free. We went inside his house and I put my road gear bag in the nice big bedroom where I'd be crashin' for the night.

Over some cold beers Ken started telling me his story. He started out as a carpenter, then became a pattern maker, then got into casting manifolds, exhausts and intakes, for farm equipment and even a few semi 18 wheelers. And then his business just took off beyond his wildest dreams. So here he is, out in the woods in a fantastic mansion with a gorgeous wife and lots of vintage Corvettes. No wonder he's so happy. Who wouldn't be?

It was already getting to be close to evening time cuz I had lost 2 hours on the flight with the time difference. But before it got dark, Ken said we should go do a test ride in the 64. OK, here we go. I got in the car in the driver's seat and first thing I noticed was,....

..................it had carpet and the seats were bolted down, I pushed myself back in the driver's seat to adjust it to drive, and I started laughing cuz the seat was bolted to the floor. Ken didn't get it. So I had to explain to him the Rat Vette I had been driving the past few years, then he got it. I actually had not driven a car with bolted down seats and carpet since September of 1981, hahaha. Yep, the White 75 I had to sell up in Wenatchee Washington was the last car I drove with carpet and bolted seats.

The test drive went awesome. The 64 was tight and solid. And it was then that Ken pointed out something that turned out to be 100% true. Folks like 4 speed Vettes cuz they drag race them and beat them and wear the shit outta the cars. This 64 here with the Power Glide only had a little over 30,000 miles on it and since it was an auto, that means most likely that nobody ever abused it like my old 63 had been. The 64 handled very well, tracked straight and true down the road, and did not have rattles and squeaks like the 63 had. So I kinda fell for the car right then and there,...even though it was an auto. I figgered if I didn't like the Power Glide by the time I got back to California, I could always sell or trade it there for a 4 speed.

Ken and Kathy grilled us up some nice T Bone Steaks for the night, then we had lots of beers. Burp. The next morning Kathy made us a big breakfast. After we ate and got cleaned up, Ken said it was time to head out. We got into his Silverado and started to back outta the garage, when he suddenly stopped, shut the truck off and sez "I forgot the juice!" He hopped outta the truck and ran back in his house. I'm sittin' there thinkin' what the hell is "the juice"?

Then Ken comes running back out with 2 six packs of beer, throws them in the back of his truck and off we go headed to Ohio, hahaha. It was probably 35 degrees or so, and that meant the beer would stay nice and cold back there, plus his truck had one of those sliding windows so you could get to the beer real easy. Now that's class, eh?

We finally got to Napoleon Ohio to see the old Vettes at Pro Team. I met Terry the owner, who I had also spoken to over the phone. Terry knew just what I was looking for and he said he had a few Sting Rays that fit my wants, mainly, them ol' 4 speed convertibles.

This picture here is inside Pro Team's showroom. These three Sting Rays were the ones I was kinda interested in,...but they were outta my price range, just like Ken said they would be. By the way, Ken and Terry seemed to know each other very well and the banter that went back and forth between them was hilarious. They were like two hungry crows getting ready to fight it out for my dead bunny rabbit carcass. Each one of them knew what I wanted in the car. Their cars came close, but none of them was perfectly what I wanted, not even Ken's White 64.

So in this line up here, that Red 63 Convertible with the hard top was also a Fuel Injected 4 speed and it had a price tag of $32,500 on it. Yikes. That would be a very high dollar car today, but for right then and there, I'da hafta keep lookin' on down the line.

That Green Convertible with the White interior is a 427 big block 4 speed car and it was $24,500. If I'da had the extra bucks, that woulda been the one to get, fun car to drive and they later went through the roof on demand.

Then the Blue Convertible down at the end was a really nice car, 327 with a 4 speed, Blue interior and it also had Factory AC in it, as you can see the AC vent in the dash. It was $22,000. Oh, and that is funny guy Ken jumping in the picture, hahaha. I guess he was the pioneer in what the kids call "Photo Bombing" today.

After I checked out Terry's nice cars with the bigger prices, Ken looked at me laughing and said "See what I mean now? Nice cars, but kinda pricey, huh?" And Terry is standing right there when Ken said that, so Terry busts in, "Dave. You said you wanted a 4 speed car, right? All these cars are 4 speeds." Ken had no rebuttal for that one. Ken's White

64 had almost everything I wanted, plus I could afford it, except it was an auto trans. I eventually told Terry he had some really nice Sting Rays for sale and I wished I could afford them, but I am a sawdust eatin' carpenter, not a crooked lawyer or rich stock broker, wink, wink.

So I went with Ken's White 64,...with the auto trans. Hmm. But it was 15,500 and I could afford that. From the 17,500 I got from the insurance, that would give me 2 grand left over, which would cover my several missed days (which means missed pay) at work and the plane ticket out to Indiana to get the car and the gas and motels for the 2,300 mile drive back home....in the dead of winter in a strange car. So maybe I'd break even? Maybe? But who knows what other terrors lie ahead out on the road back to California?

Part 86: The California Rat Years

Feb '87 Road Trip, Indiana to California

I spent the second night at Ken & Kathy's place out in the sticks in Auburn Indiana. I gave Ken the loot for his White 64 and he signed over the back of the title that evening and that was enough work for one day. The rest of the night was party,...time to eat, drink, and be merry, by bullshittin' our old Corvette war and horror stories.

The next morning bright and early after we ate breakfast, Ken was sayin' "Hey, before you head out, would ya like to go see my 57 Fuelie?" Why of course, so we jumped into his Silverado again and took off across what was basically cow pasture land, riding over dirt and not on roads, hahaha. He pulled up to a shacky little building out in the middle of nowhere and unlocked the door and there it was, a Red on Red 57 Fuelie, the Great Grand Pappy of all the Fuel Injected Corvettes, the first Holy Grail year for it.

After I am blown away by that one, he sez "Wanna go see my 65 Big Block 4 Speed?" Umm,...OK. So we took off across another wild chase and found another old building and he unlocked it and there was his 65 BIg Block, an original 396 car with 4 Speed. Then it went on and on, like 6 or 7 more times. A 63 Split Window, a 67 with 427 Tri-Power and 4 Speed, another 58 with 2 X 4s on it, a 68 Blue Big Block with 4 Speed, then a coupla more and then the last one was his 'newest' car, a Red 1970 with the LT-1 motor. I asked him "Just how many old Corvettes do you have hidden out here in the fields?" He sez "Oh,...quite a few I suppose."

Next I had to go off to downtown to the court house/city hall whatever it was and check the paperwork/registration on the car. Ken went with me in the White 64 for his Last Ride in it. I wanted everything clear and legal before I took out cross country in the Sting Ray in case I got pulled over by the red flashin' lights, if ya know what I mean?

After the legal stuff was done, then I stopped in at their auto parts store and got spare oil, a jug of antifreeze, power steering fluid, brake fluid, auto tranny fluid, windshield washer fluid, extra spark plugs, points & condenser, WD-40, and I think that's about it. I threw all of that in the back with the duffel bag.

We drove back to Ken's house and I dropped him off and said goodbye to him and Kathy, sniff, sniff. Ya know, in just two days I made really fun pals with them two, such good people. It was sad saying adios, but it was time to go. I had 2,300 miles to cover just as fast as I could.

And this was gonna be an extra easy road trip, cuz I didn't need no stinkin' map at all. All I had to do was get on I-80 West and stay on it til I pulled into the Bay Area. No turns, no exits, no detours, no nuthin', just Smoove Sailin' acrost the US of A.....in the middle of winter time.

So I hauled ass outta Indiana into Illinois, then gobbled up that state purdy quick and got into Iowa. It was getting dark by the time I got close to Des Moines, and I saw their nice old skyline lit up with the dark sky in the background. That's 500 miles down, many more to go. I kept the gas pedal down and got into Omaha, then Lincoln, the car kept running good, like it was enjoying the trip. The 64 ran straight and true down the road, the brakes worked just fine, did not pull to the left or right. I kept listening for any strange noise, but never heard anything suspicious. All's great so far.

It was after midnight when I pulled into the little gas station in Sidney, Nebraska, waaaay over on the far west side of the state, still on I-80 West. I had my map with me anyhow, just to check which towns I was passing through and to see how far I'd gone and how many more miles were left to drive. I was now just a tad over 1,000 miles from where I had started in Auburn that morning. That was pretty good time, and I was hoping to make it another 100 or 200 so I'd be about half way on the trip. If I could make the 2,300 miles in just 2 days, that would be fantastic. It was kinda funny this time having a car that not only had the seats bolted down, but also had a fuel gauge that worked, hahaha. How modern. I got the tank filled up to the top and checked the oil.

This was back in the day before paying at the gas pumps was invented, see? So that means after I filled the Sting Ray's gas tank, I had to walk into their little office, pay 'em, and then walk back out. It was on that 'Walk Back Out' part that I nearly passed out. What's that black shit on the back quarter panel of the car? OIL? Nope. Well what the fuck is it? I reached down with the fingertips of my left hand and rubbed the black stuff. Hmm. Felt funny, kinda like them old rubber pencil eraser shavings from high school days in Mechanical Drawing class. Holy shit!

RUBBER?

I backed up, focused my road bleary eyes and looked at the only rubber things on the Sting Ray. Double Fuck! The gawdamn tires are not only BALD, they got the steel belts hangin' out! HOLY SHIT! And I'd been doin' 65 or 70 on them bald puppies just minnits ago? I'm wonderin' how in the hell are they even holdin' air?

I walked back into the gas station and asked them if they got a motel around, they told me about one a few blocks into town. So there I went to get a room for the night,...or the rest of the early morning, maybe I should say? I woke up early cuz I couldn't sleep anyhow, and asked the motel lady if they had a tire store in town. She said yes. Told me where it was. I drove very gingerly, like maybe 10 mph over to the tire store, tryin' to avoid any gravel chunks bigger than a peanut. The tire store happened to be a Uniroyal shop. I was there before he opened, so I tried to catch a bit of a cat nap.

When the guy got there a few minnits later to open his shop, he came over to look at the car. I pointed out the bald-o tires to him and he kinda gasped, looked at them really close up, then busted out laughing really big, hahaha. I said "It's kinda funny and scarey at the same time, huh?" He sez, "I'm sorry. I'm not meaning to laugh at your tires, that's sad. It's just that I opened this shop here in 1969 and that was the last year those tires were made." So although those tires looked nice and new and had excellent tread on them when I left, they were still 18 year old tires that nobody told me about, and they were rotten. Today, the high dollar collector folks pay big money for them old tires like that, and I just disintegrated 'em out on I-80. Mister Tire Shop Guy fixed me up with a new set of tires so I'm off again, out into the wilderness, headed west.

This picture here is cross country road trippin' out in The Winter Time Boonies,.....somewhere the next morning. You can see on the back left corner of the car, just in front of the end of the bumper, where my fingers rubbed the old rotten tire rubber off.

Part 87: The California Rat Years

Feb '87 Road Trip, Indiana to California

Here's another shot of the 64 on its Maiden Voyage from Auburn Indiana back to San Francisco, February 1987. And yes, it was sorta cold. I liked the shadows on the front end in this shot out in the boonies.

Part 88: The California Rat Years

Feb '87 Road Trip, Indiana to California

I was a happy camper the next morning out there on the road with the new tires. And after discovering the bald tires were on their steel belts, I realized that I was very lucky that I didn't have a blow out or two while doin' 65 or 70 and wipe out the 64 in the middle of the night, wreckin' the car before I even got it home.

After leaving Sidney Nebraska with the new tires on, I continued on I-80 West. The next town of any size I saw was when I passed through Cheyenne Wyoming where my Cuzzin Paul and me had camped on that high school front porch back in 1973 on our road trip from Dallas to Canada, and that brought back some funny memories, why did we hafta sleep on the high school's front porch? Cuz there was a cattle buyers convention in town and no motel rooms for miles. Anyhow, that was back then, this is now.

The White 64 kept going west, cruisin' through Laramie and the Medicine Bow-Routt National Forest, on to Rawlins, then through Rock Springs. When I got down by Evanston, I had a flashback to the 1975 Motorsickle Road Trip with my Brudder Charles and Cuzzin Johnny when we were right here on this stretch of highway. It was very cold back then on that trip and we were drafting the 18 wheeler tryin' to stay warmer, when his right rear tire blew and flew just a coupla inches over my head. Funny how certain chunks of road can bring back memories from years before, eh?

On into Utah the 64 Sting Ray journeyed. Drove through Salt Lake City and their big salty lake, kept on going acrost Utah until I got into Nevada. It was mostly just little towns crossin' Nevada, elevations of around 4,000 feet most of the way. The Sting Ray's 300 hp 327 kept purrin' right along, kinda like it was having some fun on this trip. As for the Power Glide? I guess I was kinda gettin' used to it,......sorta,......maybe,......could be? I finally made it into Reno, which is up in the mountains out on the far west side of Nevada. And that's where I stopped for the night. That was another 1,000 miles or so. Grand Total is a bit over 2,000 miles done, under 300 miles to go.

The motel I stayed at had a nice cafe, ate there, got gas across the street and checked the oil and tranny fluid. Yep,...now I got tranny fluid to check, hahaha, never had to do that with the 63's nice ol' 4 Speed,...sigh. One thing Ken had told me was, he had gone through the car and it had all new fluids and belts. And the oil on the dipstick was still pretty clean, plus there was a door sticker on the driver's door that had the date and mileage of the last oil change. I have left that Auburn Indiana oil change sticker on there all these years, hahaha. Why not? It's part of the car's story.

Next morning, got up bright and early, ate, and hit the road again, headed on into San Francisco, which is now under 300 miles away. This photo here is outside Reno. Kinda looks like it'd make a nice magazine cover shot, don't it? And guess what? It was, hahaha. After I got the car back to California, I wrote out a letter to the editor of Vette Vues Magazine and thanked him for keeping his good magazine up and running. Told him how much I liked the mag, then I included this picture with the letter. Mentioned how the "63 Love of my LIfe" had been stolen and stripped, said how I found this unmolested original cream puff car in his magazine ads at a decent price, and told him how this 64 Convertible is now going to be the new replacement for the 63 Convertible.

Time went on by, never thought anything else about it. Then one day I got my new January 1990 Vette Vues Magazine in the mail, and,..........................

WHOA! There's this photo on its cover and a little message on the second page about the car. How's that for a lucky photo? And if ya look close at this photo, you can still see where my fingers rubbed the rubber shavings from the rotten tires off the back end, hahaha. So of course, the January 1990 issue of Vette Vues Magazine has the same finger marks on its cover. That's a story for ya right there that no drunk in the tavern would ever believe in a million years. But I was always taking pictures of things, so there ya go, it's living history now.

Part 89: The California Rat Years

Feb '87 Road Trip, Indiana to California

Now it was just a hop, skip and a jump to get from Reno back to San Francisco. I was tired, but nearly home. Covering 2,000 miles in two days is a bit of a chore. I've ridden 600 miles in a day before on the rigid chopper, so in my mind I'm tellin' myself, if I can do that shit, then I should be able to make it a 1,000 miles a day in a cushy comfortable car,... or in a vintage Sting Ray,... which ain't too cushy or comfortable, hahaha.

When I had left Auburn, I had about a 50/50 chance of either keeping or selling this 64. It had everything I liked except for the gall-dang Power Glide. If it had a 4 Speed in it, it woulda made the perfect replacement for the poor ol' 63. Sigh. But as the miles wore on with this trip, the more I liked the 64,... even with its Power Glide. It got worse mileage than the 4 Speed did, and it didn't top out as fast. (Don't ask me how I knew that cuz it was illegal.) But still, there was something about this new White Creature that really grabbed me.

I took a break at a gas station to relax a bit since I was nearly home anyhow. And the Amateur Detective in me sometimes likes to come out of hiding at certain times. This 64 is a used car. As with any and all used cars, it's Buyer Beware, you never got any clue as to what you are dealing with, right? You can't go by what anybody tells you about the car you are getting, unless they can prove they are the original owner of it. All you can do is assess what you see in front of you. So what did I see in this car now that I put a little over 2,000 miles on it?

First, the body looked totally virgin to me like it had never been in any type of wreck,.....which later turned out to be true. And then second,...those old rotten tires. The guy at the Sidney Nebraska Uniroyal tire shop told me that 1969 was the last year those tires were made. OK, let's go with that, cuz he ain't got a horse in the race, he is an unbiased source.

All the gauges in the car worked, including the odometer, which showed a bit over 30,000 miles on it. The car was sold new in 1964, the rotten tires were last made in 1969. That info kinda tells me the car was driven around 30,000 miles its first 5 years of life, then got a new set of tires and then maybe put away. Those old tires mighta been rotten, but the tread depth on 'em was still like new and the old tires even had the little teats on 'em when I got it.

So, what I am starting to realize is I mighta accidentally stumbled onto a nice unmolested virgin 64 Corvette right here in front of me. It's quiet, tight, handles good, no rattles, and since it has the cursed Power Glide, I'm guessing it was never rat raced or had anybody kinda crazy and abusive (like me) own it before. Maybe it was an old School Marm's Sting Ray, and perhaps somebody got it from her after she passed away and they stored it all these years cuz they weren't really into it? Or maybe some guy before Ken had it in his private collection and never drove it, who knows?

The correct answer is,......nobody knows, the more I drove this Power Glide car, the more I liked it. And the more I liked it, the more the pain and anguish subsided from losing the 63. Hmm,...maybe I'll keep this one? I made it on back to San Francisco with no problem whatsoever. Maybe the 64 likes me taking it out on road trips? Maybe it's been couped up for too long? Well, it ain't gonna be couped up no more. Now it's gonna go to work and haul some carpenter tools!

This photo is from when I just got back in San Francisco. See that Indiana license tag on there? I like fuckin' with cops over outta state license tags, runnin' them from other states where I don't currently live. In 1980 & 81, I ran the Texas tag on the 74 AMF Chopper when I lived in Washington, in 1983 ran the Washington tag on it when I lived in California, and later ran a California tag on the 74 AMF Chop when I lived back in Washington, in 1983 I ran the Texas tag on the 63 when I first got it to California, and now I'm running the Indiana tag in California. You should see my license tag collection in the garage. I know, lots of folks have license tag collections. What makes my collection different is they are all my tags I have run on the Choppers and Sting Rays. And I got a bunch of 'em, hahaha.

Part 90: The California Rat Years

Spring 1987 Back in Frisco

Well, lemme tell ya, I sure missed the ol' 63 Rat Vette. While the 64 is nice, it's kinda too nice for my own good. It took me awhile to get used to ridin' around on seats that were actually bolted to the dang floor. And now I even had fuckin' carpet? Eww. What a fuckin' yuppie I had become. Yikes.

Having carpet meant I had to be extra careful luggin' the carpenter tool box around now. Loadin' tools in the ol' 63, if I knocked over an open can of lacquer thinner or contact cement, all I had to do was wipe it off the bare floor before it dissolved the fiberglass, hahaha. Now with carpet, I gotta be extra careful.

And I had to be extra careful drivin' it on weekends cuz of the carpet and seat covers. It was like this,.....Ooooh, don't spill the coffee cuz it'll ruin the carpet. Ooooh, don't spill your beer down the carpet on the console, and watch out for that glowin' red cherry on the end of the joint, cuz if ya knock that thing off, then it'll burn a hole in the seat covers or carpet. Get what I mean now? This fancy 64 Vette with carpet on the dang floor was crampin' my ol' familiar Rat Style. It took me quite a while to get used to it.

I did adjust to one semi-lame thing, though. I got kinda used to the Power Glide, hahaha. Now before ya howl with laughter at me fer sayin' that and claim I was sellin' out on the 4 Speed, lemme set the stage for ya, OK? Let's say it's a fine Sunday morning in Frisco. And after you and yer Main Squeeze have a nice breakfast somewheres cuz neither one of ya is a very good cook yet, let's say you take off either up or down Highway 1 on the coast highway.

You drop the soft top down in its space back in the rear compartment behind youse two. Now ya got an open top, all the way up to the sky, just like the Beach Boys and Jan & Dean had back in the 1960s when these Sting Rays were brand fuckin' new, OK? And now you are cruisin' along with the Pacific Ocean on one side and the mountains or towns on the other side.

Now if ya were still shiftin' gears in the 4 Speed with the clutch action, you'd be very busy shiftin' back and forth as you turned all the little tight corners on the road. BUT,.....with the Power Glide, all ya gotta do is steer. And that leaves your hands free to drink your beer or Bloody Mary or Screwdriver, and you can smoke your joints with no effort. Just make sure that cherry on the end of the doobie don't burn a hole in the fuckin' carpet. This picture here is taken right where the old Silver Blue 63 used to park in Golden Gate Park, where our first joint smokin' date was, back in 1983.

And that's enough of this car crap cuz now that we're settled with the replacement car for the Stolen 63, we are headed right back into RatsVille with the 74 Rat Chop. Cuz guess what? There's another fan-fuckin'-tastic Redwood Run comin' up. And we don't wanna miss that one.

On May 24, 1987, the city of San Francisco held the 50th Anniversary for the opening of the Golden Gate Bridge. The following is taken from the archives regarding the end of the construction and the opening to the public:

"On April 27, 1937 the "Last Rivet Ceremony" was held at midspan. On May 27, 1937 Golden Gate Bridge opened to pedestrian traffic and on May 28, it opened to vehicular traffic at twelve o'clock noon, when President Franklin D. Roosevelt pressed a telegraph key in the White House to announce the event to the world. Simultaneously, every fire siren in San Francisco and Marin was sounded, every church bell rang, ships sounded their whistles, and every fog horn blew. The bridge opened ahead of schedule and under budget."

Flash forward 50 years: "On May 24, 1987, 300,000 people were stuck in human gridlock for hours while getting a rare chance to cross the 1.7-mile bridge en masse on foot to celebrate the bridge's golden anniversary. Officials quickly closed the bridge, so a half-million other people waiting to cross never got the chance. Still, the enormous, unprecedented weight caused the middle of the bridge to sag 7 feet."

"No one knows the exact weight of the pedestrians on the bridge on that May day. But assuming the average person weighs about 150 pounds and occupies about 2.5 square feet in a crowd, there would have been about 5,400 pounds for every foot in length. That's more than double the weight of cars in bumper-to-bumper traffic."

And meanwhile, up on top of Buena Vista West in the Haight Ashbury, this was the view out our living room window. At least it wasn't foggy this night. If it had been, then none of the pictures woulda turned out. The fireworks started out like a normal 4th of July celebration. But after a few minutes into it, we realized this was gonna be different.

Then we saw the Goodyear Blimp come floating in, right among the exploding fireworks. As the fireworks intensified, the sky grew wilder and wilder. It was like no fireworks display I had ever seen. The shock from the shells was coming right up into the Haight, or at least they were where we were up high.

I could feel the shock wave concussions on my face and chest. It was mesmerizing. The blasts kept increasing, the Goodyear Blimp kept floating in the exploding shells. When the Grande Finale came, the sky stayed mostly white with the big flash bomb fireworks, and everybody went nuts on the street below us and all over the city.

And that's how it went. I'm givin' ya four shots from that night, from the beginning of the fireworks show til the end, and you can see that blimp floating in there, looking like a cigar drifting in all the explosions. It kinda reminded me of the Hindenburg footage, except the Goodyear did not crash and burn.

Part 91: The California Rat Years

1987 Redwood Run

Well, I'm gonna go out on a limb now and I'm guessin' that next up on this sordid California Rat Years saga is the 1987 Redwood Run, cuz that's what the fuckin' orange ticket stub sez it is.

For the Redwood Run this time, Dave and me decided to be semi-sociable (I think that means sorta nice) and go meet the rest of the misfits and other assorted scooter trash down at the Dudley Perkins dealer for their Official Kick Off to the run. Cuz after all, it is a dealer sponsored event, and since it was our favorite run, we figgered the least we could do this year was to go ride with 'em. And with us being there on our home built choppers, it might help to add a little bit of class to their line-up goin down Highway 101, a-hem. Right? Right.

But just because we switched our meetin' place to Dudley's downtown on Page Street don't mean we switched our old routine,...puff, puff,.....cough, cough,.....as you can plainly see in this here photo, Dave and Old Yellow are right next to the 74 Rat Chop, front and center, and that means we got the two best parking spots there is, cuz we got there first-est. Early birds might get the worms, but us Early Rats get the best moldy cheese.

While Dave & me waited for the rest of the gang to show up, we went and kinda hid around this here corner and puffed ourselves up a bit. And in a few more minutes after we get The Buzz goin' good, we're gonna kick over them two Shovelhead Choppers while the rest of the guys hit their starter buttons. And then we're gonna be off, rollin' down the road, first over the Golden Gate Bridge and then on up Highway 101 to the Redwoods.

Part 92: The California Rat Years

1987 Redwood Run

Puttin' and puffin' on up HIghway 101,... we stopped in at this gas station for a little break, filled up the gas tanks, stretched the legs, and got another puff in,...or two.

Part 93: The California Rat Years

1987 Redwood Run

While the rest of the starting group from Dudleys was ridin' along nice and smooth up Highway 101, Dave and me were havin' fun being buzzed and just bouncin' along on our two rigid Shovelhead Choppers.

We eventually pulled into this 76 gas station,...maybe to have a beer or two and maybe to take a leak or two and maybe to get in another puff or two. You can never have too many puffs or beers ridin' up to a Redwood Run. And ain't this a nice Panhead Chopper we saw here? And it's got its old Mousetrap Clutch set up on it, too. It's built up kinda like Old Yellow, rigid frame, wide glide, ducktail fender on back, tin diamond primary.

Part 94: The California Rat Years

1987 Redwood Run

Dave and me bounced along Highway 101 long enough that we finally made it to French's Camp. You can see here how good Dave's 67 Old Yellow stands out in the crowd. I told Dave I am always gonna park the Rat Chop next to him so's I can find my bike when I'm wasted. A Black Chop gets lost in a sea of black bikes.

We still got the road gear on the bikes so we'd better get our asses down into The Pit and get our tent spots picked out. First we gotta ride across the bridge and give 'em our orange tickets and get our wristbands, then we are good to go for the rest of the weekend. Saturday night we get steak dinners with the ticket price and the music is gonna be the Charlie Daniels band this year.

Part 95: The California Rat Years

1987 Redwood Run

Well, here he is folks, my favorite work partner on the construction jobs and he also doubles as my favorite chopper ridin' partner. This is Dave, the creator of the San Francisco based 67 Shovel known as Old Yellow.

He's sittin' here doin' what he does best,.....drinkin' beer, smokin' joints, sittin' on his 67 Genny Shovel Chopper he built himself, wearing his brand spankin' new Redwood Run T Shirt. What more could ya ask for, hahaha? And just lookit that big shit eatin' grin he has goin' on, I bet he's high right now. Dang, I sure miss this funny guy and them olden days.

And hey, just wait a gawddam minnit, I don't see the Black Rat Chop anywhere in this photo. Does that mean Dave moved Old Yellow and is tryin' to ditch me?

Part 96: The California Rat Years

1987 Redwood Run

Here's some hoodlums that were camped right next to us. I can't remember their names but they were some fun folks. I bet they could be going after more cold frosty beer. What do you think? The gal in front seems to be the only one with a beer, and hers might be gettin' warm, who knows?

Part 97: The California Rat Years

1987 Redwood Run

OK now, you might be askin' yourself just what the fuck is this picture of and what the hell is it about? Well simmer down some and I'll tell ya. Well, ya see it's like this. When ya go to the Redwood Runs, you gotta smoke dope all the time yer there cuz this is the area in Northern California where it grows good and ya gota be patriotic, see? Ya gotta be cool like WIllie Nelson and support your local farmers, cuz it's the right thing to do.

OK, so once you been smokin' the good bud for a few minnits, next thing ya know you got what they call Severe Cotton Mouth. When ya get Severe Cotton Mouth, there is only one cure for it and that is ice cold frosty beers. So ya go get them beers and ya slug 'em down, see? And since they taste sooo good ya keep drinkin' 'em and ya keep drinkin' 'em some more, one right after the other, until ya gotta go pee. See? Now that is where this photo comes in.

I went into the Porto-John and whilst I was takin' a leak, I took this picture lookin' out that little slit window they have on top of the outhouses. Ya might say multi-taskin' was invented like this. So there ya have it. That's what this picture is. And I'll bet this is the only photo like this that you have seen,....today. Right? I knew it........

Part 98: The California Rat Years

1987 Redwood Run

This picture here was taken by my ridin' patner Dave. Now ol' Dave was a fantastic ridin' partner and a good carpenter and a good mechanic and a wonderful husband and pop, but he wasn't all that great at getting the pictures just right all the time, but he tried like the dickens.

As you can see, this here is just kind of a weird picture of me and the motor homes behind me. Dave totally missed the Rat Chop in the photo. But one thing he did get is the Miller Beers. If you ever notice, you will hardly ever (if never) see a photo of me at a run with just one beer. I always gots to have lots of beers. And if ya think them beers get warm on me at the runs, then you ain't never seen me swaller them. I can slug 'em down purdy fast.

Part 99: The California Rat Years

1987 Redwood Run

This is one of the dirt roads that goes around the perimeter of French's Campground. There's no parking meters or meter maid cops here, either, so come and get a parking spot for free. Maybe you might even see your bike in the row? (If you are an old fart, that is.)

Part 100: The California Rat Years

1987 Redwood Run

This is the 74 Rat Chop with my Miller Beers hangin' on the handlebars and me eatin' my steak in the dirt. For years, I have blabbed and blabbed and written about the awesome steak dinners the Redwood Run would grill up for us. They always smelt and tasted so great. And yet I never got a picture of one of 'em.

So I sez to Dave, "Hey, can ya take the camera and go stand over there and take a picture of our steak dinners?" So he moved back a few feet and this is the picture he got, hahaha. Of course, I didn't know he was kinda drunkish and missed the entire steak photo until we got back home and I got the pictures developed. Oh well, this is kinda close,...sorta. And next up, after we eat, the Charlie Daniels Band is gonna be on stage.

Part 101: The California Rat Years

1987 Redwood Run

And then Saturday night we got to see Charlie Daniels Band right in front of us. What's better than being all wasted out in the dirt and getting to see and hear Charlie play? He played his Les Paul and Magic Fiddle into the dark hours.

Part 102: The California Rat Years

1987 Redwood Run

Whew! Few things are worse than a Sunday Mornin' Hangover at the Redwood Runs, hahaha. Ears were ringin' from Charlie Daniels and straight pipes, so that was good cuz it blew out all the cobwebs.

Dave, Kent & Lori and me rode into town and ate breakfast. Then before we packed up the tents and headed back home, we rode through the Redwoods one last time. If this ain't the most perfect road in the world to ride motorsickles on, then I don't know what is.

Part 103: The California Rat Years

1987 Redwood Run

One last shot of our little group in the huge Redwoods. I set the Canon down on a log, set the timer for 10 seconds and then ran over to the others. "Click"

See how that 67 Shovelhead Old Yellow stands out? And now it's time to ride back to camp and roll up our gear and start ridin' back to the Bay Area. Chalk up another fun Redwood Run. And none of us caught on fire or had our bike frames break, hahaha.

Part 104: The California Rat Years

1987 Redwood Run

One last beer and weed stop on Highway 101 leavin' the 1987 Redwood Run. This might be at The Keg, can't tell for sure. And maybe your bike is in the crowd?

Part 105: The California Rat Years

1987 Redwood Run

This was a gas stop on the way back to the Bay Area. I saw that cop standing there like that, doin' nuthin' so I told Kent, "Hey I'm gonna go stand by the cop like he just cuffed me" and then Lori jumped in and said "I'm going with you." So she's lookin' at me like 'what the fuck didya do this time?' And the cop never had any clue of what we were doing. That's the 74 AMF Chop and Dave's Old Yellow behind us.

Part 106: The California Rat Years

1987 Redwood Run

And here's our last gas stop photo before we all split up to go our separate ways,...sniff, sniff. We got here Dave and Old Yellow, the 74 Rat Chop and looks like a Hessians MC member over there with the mousetrap set up on his nice ol' road chopper.

Part 107: The California Rat Years

Fall 1987 Busted!

So fall of 1987 rolled around and you'll never believe the hilarious shit that went down! Remember the poor ol' Silver Blue 63 Sting Ray that got ripped off and stripped in December 1986? The one that I played detective and went out searchin' for its murderers and took all them photos and gave to the cops? And then the lazy cops never did nuthin' about it? Well, about the same time that the 63 Vette got ripped off from me, Rick had another customer from his Corvette shop that had a Black 1964 Convertible. I forget that other customer guy's name, so we'll just call him "Bob" for this story, OK?

Bob's Black 1964 Sting Ray also got ripped off about the same time my 63 did. Unlike my situation where the cops found my car's carcass two days later, they never found Bob's Sting Ray carcass, his was just missin' from then on. He never got "closure" like I did. So on a fine Saturday morning in the fall of '87, Bob has his wife's car down at a local muffler shop in Frisco getting some exhaust work done. Over up on the lift next to his wife's car is a Red Sting Ray Convertible, either a 63 or 64, they kinda look the same from a distance, and since it's up on the lift Bob can't see the hood to tell the difference in years and he also can't see the gauges.

So for all intentions of this funny saga, it's either a 63 or 64 and ya can't tell which year just yet. Ya gotta be able to see the hood or gauges to tell 'em apart, or you can tell 'em apart by their hubcaps, but this car had mags on it, no stock hubcaps. So it is a Mystery Year Sting Ray for right now.

But,……..Bob recognizes something about the Red Sting Ray's undercarriage that he recognizes, and he discovers that is HIS frame up on the lift. (See where this is going now?) There is a young Mexican kid with the car, maybe mid 20s? The first thing Bob does is to keep quiet, and he goes to the phone in the office and makes two very important phone calls, yep, first Bob calls the coppers, then he calls Rick from the Corvette shop. Bob tells the cops and Rick that he has most definitely found his stolen car from last December. Then Rick calls me and I went down to witness all this funny shit. Luckily this all happened on a Saturday or I woulda been at work.

By the time I get down there to the muffler shop, the funny questioning has already been going on for a while and Bob is fuckin' PISSED like I was and the cops are grillin' the kid, but good. The kid looks like he is ready to start cryin', why? Cuz them mean ol' cops that showed up to check out the Red Sting Ray asked the little booger kid for his registration papers,...and,... guess what? He ain't got none! And I'm just standin' there watchin' and lovin' this funny shit. While the cops were still questioning the kid, and while Bob was mad as fuckin' hell, Rick filled me in on the first part of their questioning that I missed.

When the cops had asked the kid for papers to his car, he said he ain't got any. Ooops. Then they noticed he ain't got a legal license tag. Ooops again. And then they found out the kid ain't got no legal driver's license,......oops, again. Then the cops said they were gonna run the kid into jail and told him he was gonna be going off to prison big time for grand auto theft. The kid kept sayin' he did not steal the car,...which maybe was true. Cuz the guys I took the pictures of were probably in their 30s and 40s. But the cops still have him for being in possession of stolen property.

And then it gets even funnier. The cops and Rick and Bob walk up to the Red Sting Ray still up on the lift, and they took a flat blade screwdriver and lightly scratched the Red paint on the car, and guess what happened? Underneath the fairly fresh Red paint on the body was Bob's Black paint. Oh dear. And underneath the Red paint on the doors was my Silver Blue paint. Oh my goodness, what have we here? The thieves took Bob's 64 Sting Ray and my 63 Sting Ray and they made this unregistered combination Sting Ray out of both of our cars.

So now the kid knows he's busted and he knows the two legal owners of both the stolen Sting Rays are right there 10 feet away from him, fuckin' mad as hell, ready to fuckin' kill him with our bare hands if the cops weren't there to protect his lyin' ass. And once the cops tell him he'd better start squealin' on the thieves, the singin' canary kid broke down and started cryin' and blabbin', so the coppers took him off downtown for 'further questioning.'

The stool pigeon kid wound up spillin' his guilty guts. He told the cops everything, the thieves' names and where they lived and the shop address where they were running their car theft ring, and when the cops did their raid on that car theft ring shop, they busted the goons with a brand new stolen Chevy truck with a hydraulic tail gate, and they got busted with a new Toyota pick up with a hydraulic tail gate, cuz the thieves use those hydraulic units for their lowriders, see? But wait, it gets even better.

The asshole thieves also got busted with a stolen brand fuckin' new bright yellow AAA Tow Truck! That's right. They had ripped off the brand spankin' new AAA Tow Truck and were using that to go around San Francisco, rippin' off cars right in broad daylight in front of all kinds of witnesses. Cuz in a big city like that, folks are used to seeing cars get towed off all the damn time, right? So these crooks had it made, swipin' new cars in front of everybody, probably swipin' cars right in front of other cops, too. But now,...they'z busted.

And the Happy Ending is, they all went off to San Quintin to cool their hot thievin' heels for a while. I hope they enjoyed lots and lots of forced receptive anal sex in the joint, cuz they deserve it. I just love happy endings.

This happier day's picture here is 'In Memory' of the ol' 63 Sting Ray that I loved so dearly, sniff, sniff. Rick eventually rebuilt this car and then sold it to a cop that lived in Oakland. I got it from a cop in Irving Texas and then it went back with a cop in Oakland. So I guess it's a "1963 Cop Car" now.

Part 108: The California Rat Years

Fall 1987

As 1987 came to a close, the ol' 74 Rat Chop was startin' to leak a bit,...or well,...maybe it was startin' to leak a lot. Oil was leaking outta the tranny shaft seal, outta the bottom of the kicker cover and outta the bottom of the engine cases and a few other little secret spots it didn't want me to know about. The awesome Joe Cox stroker motor build from 1979 had served me well, but it was now showin' its mileage. The rebuild wasn't all that old in years, but I think all the miles I had put in criss crossin' the nation kinda did it in. But at least I had me some fun wearin' that ol' motor out.

One day after work I came out to the Rat Chop where I had parked it in one of the legal bike parkings spots on the end of the row. But while I was walking up to it, I noticed it was over maybe 2 feet from where I had left it. When I got to it, there was a note on the seat tucked under the cable lock. It was a SF Muni bus driver's time card and he had left a note saying he had accidentally hit the bike while he was turning the corner. Long story short, I wound up telling James Perkins about it at Dudley's, so he wrote me up an estimate of the damage and I mailed in the claim form. A few weeks later I got a letter from then SF Mayor Feinstein and a check for $512, I think it was. So, I got to fix a few dents.

On the Sting Ray side of things, the thieves who ripped off the 63 were enjoyin' their nice free vacation in the Gray Bar Hotel Quintin. And the 64 was filling in as a nice substitute, even though it had the Power Glide auto tranny. We'd occasionally take the 64 to drive-in car shows to places like Mel's Diner out in the Avenues close to the ocean, or maybe we'd venture up to wine country at the drive-in car shows like the one at Korbel winery, the folks who make my favorite Brandy.

And it seems where ever we took that White 64, some folks would come up and always start to say shit like 'nice car' but then they'd look inside and see it was an automatic. So then I'd get comments like "Where's the other pedal?" "You got a lady's car?" "Nice car, but too bad it's a Power Glide." "Why would anyone wanna drive a Sting Ray without a 4 speed?"

I got used to their lame bad mouthin' shit, hahaha. Flash forward to these days. Now at car shows all the old farts wanna buy it. Why? Cuz they got bad knees, they've had funky knee replacements, they got bad hips and bad feet, can't work the clutch pedal no more,... awww,...sniff, sniff. Well, guess what suckers? You made fun of the ol' Power Glide back then. And now you find out only 8% of the Sting Rays in 1964 had Power Glides. And suddenly what used to be my semi-embarrassment is now your highly desired ultra rare option? Oh well, too bad. I'll keep cruisin' in the 64 with the PG and they can keep using their sore legs on their clutch pedals and then they can go suck a bag of dicks, how's that one, hah?

On the home front, we were still kicked back in the itty bitty Haight Ashbury Penthouse, cramped as it was. Killer view, but very small space. And when the fog came in, there was no view at all. But at least nuthin' else was gettin' stolen at the time.

And then on the job front, I started what turned out to be one of my favorite jobs of all time,...building the new Nordstroms store down on Market Street, downtown San Francisco. I'd ride the oil drippin' leaky Rat Chop to work. And after it got hit in the legal bike parking spots, I started parkin' it on the sidewalk at the job site and the Rat Chop never got a single ticket.

The company I went to work for was from Seattle. The Big Boss Man Superintendent was a great guy named Jim, his Assistant Super was a helluva nice guy named Gale, their General Foreman was a good smart guy named Gary, and I came in Number 4 on their Pecking Order as the Head Lay Out Dude. This was a gravy job. Being the Lay Out Guy is a fun job, as long as you know what you're doing. Cuz if you fuck it up, everybody on the whole damn job knows you fucked it up. Luckily, I never had any fuck ups. Lay out work is like buildin' a chopper. Always double check and triple check every move you make,...to avoid future embarrassment.

What was so different and special about this construction job? Well, since you didn't ask, here goes: The 8 Storey building is gonna have Spiraling Escalators. Yep, that's correct. Escalators that are gonna spiral as they go up and down. This is gonna be only the third set of these things in the world, and the other two sets are in Japan. The total building height is 8 floors, and Nordstroms is taking the top 5 floors, while other various shops will have the bottom 3 floors. The bottom 3 floors will have the spiraling escalators and the Nordstrom part on the top 5 floors will have criss-cross escalators which take off up through the giant atrium above the spiraling ones. It was quite a mechanical feat, for sure.

There is a big oval opening in the center of all the floors, an atrium going from the bottom of the lowest floor to the ceiling and roof on top. It turned out to be spectacular, if I don't mind sayin' so myself. Today you can Google or Youtube the Nordstrom Spiraling Escalators and see how they work. And they were made by Fujitec, from Japan, and their entire Fujitec installation crew was from Japan.

Maybe the architect's idea on this design of this building was to rival the Neiman Marcus store's 7 floor Rotunda atrium at their entrance? I dunno. All I know is the Nordstrom store was gonna have one helluva huge hole going all the way up to the top, and it was up to us guys to make it all work. And now, 32 year old Nasty Rat Chop rider me gets to be the only guy in the universe that got to work on both the Neiman's Rotunda woodwork and then lay out the Nordstroms Spiraling Escalators. Oh my,.....

Around the entire atrium floor, all the escalator openings were going to land on radiused marble floors, laid out in colored concentric patterns. Nordstroms was spending $7 million on the Italian marble floors alone and not only was all the marble flooring gonna be from Italy, but so was their crew. They did not speak English and I do not speak Italian, we had to have a translator on the job.

I worked with the architects and engineers. Using the old-fashioned Tripod & Instrument, I established 4 main permanent points on each floor. Those 4 points in the concrete floor were our Ground Zero starting points and from those, I'd anchor my string line and swing the big radiuses and mark them on several sheets of plywood laid on the floor. (Are ya still with me?) Then I'd make plywood templates for each radius size.

By cutting just one radius in one sheet, that would give you two halves, see? So, you got an inside radius and the other piece left over would be your outside radius. We needed both pieces to spray paint the radiuses on the floor for the marble flooring guys to follow. I will admit it was scary at first, getting the templates perfect. No slip ups allowed.

But once we proved they worked on the first floor, then all I had to do was go up through the building, use the 4 points on each floor to start from, and do the same layouts on each floor. That is where the Gravy Part came in. Well, sorry I rambled so much about this boring work stuff, but these were the first spiraling escalators in the USA, only the third set in the entire world, and I was one of the very few guys that made it all happen. I'm kinda proud of that job.

This rainy picture here is Lay Out Dude me on the Nordstrom jobsite. I got on this job when it was just bare concrete floors sticking up in the air. I also laid out all the perimeter walls, which is what I'm doing in this picture. I set the Canon AE-1 camera on the floor and set the timer and there ya go. That is Powell Street in the background. This new Nordstroms building is across the street from where the cable cars turn around to head back the other way up Powell Street. It's one of the more famous intersections in the City by the Bay. And this view no longer exists cuz the solid exterior wall to Nordstrom's is there, so ya can't see shit. This might be the only photo with bare floors and no walls like this.

Part 109: The California Rat Years

February 1988

Things started changing in San Francisco, as in...things started getting worse, in my humble point of view. Prices on everything were going up, and old familiar places that used to be really cool and fun hangouts were now getting either commercialized, yuppie-fied, or even knocked down by the bulldozers and wreckin' balls.

Livin' on top of The Haight had been such a blast, but they even started changin' that, too. We used to go ridin' or drivin' over the top of Twin Peaks to an old timey 1930s-type grocery store on the other side out on Market Street, and it was called Tower Market. Twin Peaks made doing mundane shit like gettin' groceries and beer kinda fun. The top of Twin Peaks used to be just wind, dirt and weeds, totally original, unmolested. It was a really cool place to go to unwind and there was hardly ever anyone there.

Twin Peaks was the cool old place where Oakland Steve and me used to ride up, so we could go get high up on top of the world, back when I first rode the 74 AMF Chopper into town in the summer of 1982. Now they were starting to ruin this place as well.

The commercial interests were takin' over and they poured concrete everywhere and put up the concrete retaining walls and next thing ya know? Tour buses are everywhere going up and coming down from Twin Peaks. They made a massive parking lot on top for the buses to unload the tourists and they even had stupid gift shop crap and food vendors for them to buy dumb shit. So, you can no longer do things like this.

What do I mean by "this"? Just simple shit, really, like sittin' in a 1964 Sting Ray convertible, top down, smokin' a fat joint, listenin' to a real rock & roll radio station, lookin' out over The City Lights waaay down below. Those days are now gone. This spot here is now ruined...forever.

Part 110: The California Rat Years

Then Came 1988

And here we've got an old photo that nobody has ever seen before cuz I never let anyone see it until right now, how's that for ya'll bein' all special an' shit?

I took this picture from the north side of the Nordstroms store, standing right out on the edge of the concrete slab, riskin' my pathetic life, mind ya. And this view does not exist today cuz they finished the walls on the store a few weeks after I took this photo.

This incredible view (if I don't mind sayin' so myself) is lookin' right up the guts of Powell Street. And not only is it the famous corner right where the cable cars turn around, I even got a cable car in the photo, turnin' around just for you. And like I said, nobody has ever seen this photo before, cuz it is recently untombed from my old photo albums I keep in the dungeon for special occasions such as this one.

That building to the right of the cable car used to be the old Woolworth Building, and my Oklahoma farm girl mom worked inside that Woolworth store while my dad was in the Navy, stationed at Treasure Island during WW 2. (That was the other war, to end all wars.)

Part 111: The California Rat Years

Spring 1988

If any of you remember the stories from The Early Years, 1973 to 1979, this is Ray, my ol' Dallas ridin' partner I met in 1974,....the hard and brutal way. Ray is the guy that bought the custom 1972 Super Glide out from under me at Ivey's Harley dealer in Texas at the end of June. My Dream '72 Super Glide already had the front end kicked out 6 inches, still had the good ol' Sportster drum brake wheel on it and was runnin' the ol' fat bob tanks. The 72 was painted Black with Red Pinstripes. I was in love with it. It was for sale for 2,500 bucks, 600 cheaper than the new piece of crap I wound up with. And I had cash from selling the ol' 67 Sportster and was ready to buy that 72 Glide.

When I got down to the dealer with the money,......the 72 Shovelhead was GONE! That's right, so I still ain't got no bike to ride until the fateful day of July 11, 1974 when I got the 74 AMF. So it is Ray's fault that I got cursed with the 74 that was built during the middle of the Summer of 1974 AMF Strike.

As if having a bike bought out from under you ain't bad enough, when I was driving my 68 Mustang up my own damn street, there was that Black 72 Super Glide, sittin' out in the yard in front of one of my neighbor's houses. Damn! I walked up and knocked on the door to see who it was that bought my dream bike out from under me, and this guy right here answered the door, hahaha. Turned out he was my neighbor, newly wed to Debra, (they are still hitched today), and a coupla weeks later after I got the Cursed 1974 Super Glide, we all became instant riding partners.

So even though I did not get the bike of my dreams, at least I got to ride along beside it and watch it going down the road with my new best friends on it. OK, now to this picture up on the Penthouse roof. Ray was also a carpenter and we worked together on jobs. Ray & Debra still lived in Dallas and the company Ray was working for had a little job to do in Hawaii. So they were flying Ray from Dallas to Hawaii, and San Francisco was the stop along the way. Ray called me up on the phone from Dallas before he left, and he told me he had to change planes here, and he had a whole whoppin' 5 hour layover. So the special day came and he landed in San Francisco,...for 5 hours only.

So I hurried down to the airport and picked him up in the ol' Sting Ray and drove him back to Frisco and we did a convertible whirlwind tour with the top down, saw the Pacific Ocean, Golden Gate Park, drove him over the Golden Gate Bridge and then we came back through the Haight. While we were drivin' up Haight Street going back to our shack on top of the hill, we stopped at the intersection on Haight at Masonic to let the pedestrians walk on by.

While we were sitting there, this gen-u-ine old hippie dude, complete with multi colored cotton parka, comes moseyin' by. He had on big faded bell bottom jeans, sandals, the hippie parka, and a big ol' floppy leather hat like Billy wore in Easy Rider. When the hippie got in front of the Sting Ray, he stopped, looked at us, then he smiled really big and bowed with his arms outstretched like he was on stage takin' a bow in front of the audience that was givin' him a standing ovation. And then he leaned over and kissed the Sting Ray right on its nose emblem, then he raised back up and proceeded on acrost the street. Ray and me busted out laughing, hahaha. Then I looked at Ray and said "I bet you never had that happen to you in Dallas, didya?" Ray said no.

So we came on up the Buena Vista hill and went up into the little Penthouse and had some Champagne and I fired up some of that green sticky stuff to celebrate Ray's trip and his San Francisco Layover. I saw Ray and Debra a few years ago at my dad's funeral and Ray was one of my dad's pall bearers. Ray & Debra,...I love ya'll and thanks for your long time friendship and fun memories.

(But I'm still semi-pissed off that you got that 1972 Super Glide before I got to it, wink, wink.)

Part 112: The California Rat Years

Spring 1988

This here is our ex-kid, Wally. I know, I know,... he don't look like neither one of us. That's what happens sometimes. Mailman? Postman? Weedman? Likker Store Dude? Who knows how it happent?

Wally was sort of a problem child, maybe a juvenile delinquent? He was raised in the jungle down in South America. Maybe he had been a gang member, I got no clue. We got him at a place that sold feathered things like this. Wally had a band on his leg. The guy that ran the shop said that band had a registered number that proved Wally was a legally caught critter.

But I think that band mighta actually been a monitoring band cuz he mighta been on work release. We put up with Wally for 6 whole fuckin' noisy ass years. But he got soooo fuckin' loud that some building landlord creeps in Seattle eventually told us he was too loud, and not fit to live in an apartment. And since we couldn't afford a house, we were apartment dwellers and had to adjust.

That means Wally went off to go live at the Napa Feather Farm back down in California, which I guess turned out to be OK for him. He got to live up on top of a big hill, overlooking vineyards, and he got to scream all he wanted plus he got to breed with the female critters and they got to produce offspring. Still, I look back at the old photos like this one, and I remember how much fun he had screamin' and flappin' his big wings up on top of the Penthouse wall.

He'd walk back and forth on this wall with the wind blowing his feathers every direction. Then he'd just scream and scream and scream and scream. He thought it was funny making racket, kinda like we all do makin' our own racket with straight pipes. He was just tryin' to have some fun, that's all. Wally, we still miss you. Hope you didn't get burnt up in a wildfire in Napa. And if ya did get burnt up, I just wonder,.....didya taste like chicken?

Part 113: The California Rat Years

Spring 1988

Now we got us here one last job picture from building the Nordstroms store and there's two job stories to go with it cuz they happened on the same day. And then we're gonna go smack dab into the 1988 Redwood Run, so beware.

Story 1: Doing the layout work for the radiused marble floors and all the rest of the perimeter walls in the entire building was an easy job after I got the radiused templates made and figgered out on the first floor. So the nice boss man gave me a brand new First Year Apprentice to work with me doing the rest of the 7 floors. His name was Mike, probably 23 or 24, and his wife Lisa also worked for this same construction company, in the office with the big bosses. And this entire company and Mike & Lisa were all from Seattle. So although the job is physically in San Francisco, I still felt like the odd guy out cuz they all knew each other from Seattle and I was "the new guy" if ya get what I mean?

There was this Lez-bean Ironworker Apprentice on the job. She wore more tools than any 2 or 3 other regular guy Ironworkers. Ya know how on Gunsmoke or Have Gun Will Travel, Matt Dillon and Paladin always wore just one gun, but they were really good and fast with it? And ya remember how when a bad guy gunslinger came to Dodge City, sometimes he'd be wearin' two pistols? And he'd be walkin' bow-legged with his arms spread out over the two pistols? Well that's the way this Lez-beam Ironworker gal was. She'd go walking along with her arms spread out and you'd hear all her many tools jinglin' as she walked, just like Festus' spurs on Gunsmoke.

"Jing-jing-jing-jing-jing" you'd hear her comin' and goin'. So on this particular day, Mike and me were down on the floor close to where this picture was taken. We were scratching our layout marks into the concrete floor with our diamond point stainless steel scratchers. Then we'd spray whatever color code we needed for the Italian marble floor guys to use, then we'd spray a clear coat over that color to protect it.

So as we are spraying the clear coat paint, we hear her comin', "jing, jing, jing, jing, jing" as she walked on past us. Mike is lookin' up at her as she moseys on by, all bow legged like she just got off her horse with her arms all spread out like an eagle ready to take off. Then Mike looks at me with a grin and sez, "She looks like she's thinking to herself, if I had a cock, it'd be HUGE!" And we both busted out laughing and she turned around to look at us, but she never knew what Mike said,......until right now. Don't go tell her, OK? Just keep it between us right here.

Story 2: When it got to be lunch time, if it was nice weather, a bunch of us in the crew would venture outside across Market Street to the little square where the cable cars turned around. They had these nice long benches, maybe 12 to 16 feet long, where folks would sit and eat or smoke or drink coffee or read their newspapers.

One of the guys in our crew, big heavy guy named Don, was down at the end of the bench. His work partner Pete was next to him, then Mike was there and then I was on the other side of Mike. And on the left hand side of me was this really ritzy looking rich lady. She was all dressed up like she was a business executive who made the Big Bucks. You could tell her clothes cost boo-koo moolah and she had on flashy jewelry that was real sparkly in the sun.

All of a sudden, with no warning, while we are eatin' our sammitches, this "lady" got up from the bench, took maybe 2 or 3 steps forward and a couple to our right to where she is standing right in front of all four of us, and she's facing us. And then?

And then she kinda hikes up her fancy dress a bit, squats down right in front of us and starts peein' right while we are eatin', she's squatted down, pissin' like a cow on a flat rock, just going everywhere, and grinnin' at us while she's doing it. So we got up and left and went to another bench. And that's life in San Francisco, them two stories oughta get ya warmed up for the 1988 Redwood Run, cuz it's next up on the agenda. This is a picture of one of the escalator landings. And yes, since I'm a chopper guy, I put them fancy pinstripes on my hard hat.

Part 114: The California Rat Years

Awwright, Now It's the 1988 Redwood Run

The 1988 Redwood Run got off to a hectic start for our little crew. The panic actually set in the Thursday night before we were to leave Friday morning. What was The Panic? We had run outta weed! Dave was totally out and bone dry, I had only a few little chunks left, about enough to roll up one little skinny sad joint,...maybe. What the fuck were we gonna do without weed for the Redwood Run? Then, later that night, this guy I know may or may not have called me up and maybe did or did not tell me he mighta had or not had some sticky green bud in. Whew. So maybe I got it.

I called up Dave and told him to not worry, we were set. As you can tell from this goofy photo, this was not a normal Redwood Run take off. Dave, Kent & Lori and me were not meeting at the Golden Gate Bridge like we had in years past, and we were not meeting at Dudley Perkins for the official start, either. So where were we? I forget. But here we are, out in some big ass parking lot somewhere in downtown San Francisco.

The deal was, this was 1988 and that meant it was Harley Davidson's 85th Birthday, so they were having a Birthday Bash, complete with a big white cake. And Vaughn Beals, the President of Harley Davidson and some other Big Wigs, were up there blabbing on the stage about how great they were doing. Yawn. Is it time for the big group to pull out yet? Seemed like we were never gonna get to leave. Why were we doing this thing? Cuz Harley is the one that sponsors the run, so we figgered it was the least we could do.

And there was this TV Nooze Crew there, and out of all the goons in the parking lot they had to choose from, they picked my goonie ass and the nasty oil slingin' Rat Chop to come interview. They came right up to me and the 74 AMF and were asking me dumb questions like did I think that home made bike of mine would make it? They asked me if I thought I could make it all the way there to the campground without it breaking down? They asked why didn't I ride a normal lookin' bike like the other guys rode? Why don't they go bug somebody else?

I was like,...sheesh! Gimme a fuckin' break already. So, I pulled out my own damn camera and started asking them dumb questions, like did they know who their real daddy was? I asked them if they really paid somebody cash money to fuck up their hair like that? I asked them why don't they go get a real job, loading boxes into trucks down at UPS or something like that? Then I said let's see YOU guys build up a bike and try to ride it all the way to French's Campground without it breaking down. And then they walked away from me,...for some reason. Some folks ain't got no sense of humor, eh?

So once the fuckin' yuppie news crew was gone, I called Dave over and showed him what I had scored the night before. After I got the whole bag for 400 clams Thursday night, I took it home and got out my little dangly ball weight and split it into two baggies, one for Dave, one for me. Now we are set for the 1988 Redwood Run to kick off. Right after we did a big ol' puff, that is. I stuck my baggie of fun into my leather jacket pocket. Dave stuck his baggie into his jacket pocket. Now we're almost ready to kick the choppers over and take off. Almost.

Part 115: The California Rat Years

1988 Redwood Run

OK, after we got rid of the TV Nooze Crew, we did the Big Puffs to set everything just right in our noggins, then we were ready to roll outta there,...where ever this is. I stil don't remember, hahaha. That's my riding/work partner Dave on the far left, Lori in the middle, and me with Dave's 67 Shovel Chop Old Yellow behind me and the leaky oil slingin' 74 Rat Chop over behind Dave. Photo is by Kent, our fellow carpenter at work, who also got to take off early for the Redwood Runs, yay.

Part 116: The California Rat Years

1988 Redwood Run, And We're Off!

After hagglin' with the TV crew for a while, and finally getting our weed situation under control, we were eventually able to kick over them choppers and take off up Highway 101 headed to yet another Redwood Run.

Since this 'official start' took longer than we planned and a lot longer than the other runs we had been on, that means we got a semi-late start. So that also means we stopped along the way for some grub, beer, and puffs. And this was our first stop. We peeled off from the big group we were ridin' with and pulled into this joint. I had one of their dee-lish-shush Bar-be-que sammitches. Don't remember what the others et.

At this 1988 Run, Kent & Lori had traded in their old Sportster and got the new Blue Beauty up above on the left side. Then we got the Black Rat in the center and Dave's Old yellow on the right end to round out the effect at the Mom & Pop Joint. Wonder if it's still there today?

I was havin' fun gettin' all high an' laughin' and jokin' an' shit until we walked outside to the bikes and I saw what had happened to the leaky oil slingin' 74 Rat Chop. Bummer.

Part 117: The California Rat Years

1988 Redwood Run Bummer!

So due to all the TV crew interview crap and all the other blabbernouth wind-bag guest speaker shenanigans and other mind bogglin' hoopla they had thrown before leaving for this Official Start to the 1988 Redwood Run,..... we got off to a later start than normal. And that means we were on the road up on HIghway 101 later than normal. And that means we were stopping to eat lunch at the little Mom & Pop place which we had never done before. Breakfast? Maybe. Lunch? Never.

But the food and beer was good so what the hell, right? And then we came back out to the bikes. And that's when I noticed that the back tire on the 74 Rat Chop was kinda flat-ish lookin', but only on the bottom, great, just fuckin' great. What a fun way to start our Redwood

Run. A late start and now a fuckin' flat tire. Luckily, I was always prepared for funny shit like that and I had a can of Fix A Flat with me.

I was laughing with Kent & Lori and I asked Dave to take a picture of the flat tire and unlucky me. So Dave grabbed my camera and took this 'wonderful' photo, except he never got the flat tire part in, and I didn't know he had missed the flat bottom of the tire in the photo until a few days later when I got the film developed.

Oh well, that's the way it goes. Sometimes Dave missed the main part of photos, but what the hell? At least he tried and did get part of it and there's the can of Fix A Flat. Let's air that flat tire up and hit the road,....right after we do another puff or three.

Part 118: The California Rat Years

1988 Redwood Run On the Way

So far this 1988 Redwood Run seemed to be fulla goblins and gremlins. First off, we had massive trouble gettin' some green sticky skunk weed for the run, just barely got an ounce a few hours before take off. Then we had all that bally-hoo at the launch cuz it was Harley's 85th Birthday Bash and them Harley Executives from Milwaukee gave us a late start for the birthday present cuz they just had to keep congratulatin' each other on how wonderful they were.

And if all that ain't bad enough, when Kent & Lori and Dave and me came outta the Mom & Pop diner at lunch time, I had a fuckin' flat on the back tire. At least the can of Fix A Flat shit worked for the duration of the run. We headed on up Highway 101 toward the Redwoods and eventually pulled into another spot to get some gas and a beer and to smoke some more green bud just in case the buzz might wear off before we got to French's Campground, hahaha. And there was this crunchy gravel big parking lot that had this wonderful Panhead contraption in it. So now things are startin' to look up a little bit.

Part 119: The California Rat Years

Goofy 1988 Redwood Run

After fixin' the 74 Rat Chop's flat with the can of Super Duper Spray A Tire Shit, we proceeded on our merry way up to the Redwoods. One terrible thing stands out HUGE in my memory on this ride up, though, and anyone on a rigid can relate, I'm sure. Didya ever hit a bump soooooo fuckin' huge that you still remember it 34 years later? Well,...we did. Dave and me usually rode toward the back of a pack of bikes. I always liked looking up the row from the tail end, listenin' to the pipes talk in front of us, and seeing all the different types and colors of bikes snakin' along the road, see? It was kinda like being in a an ol' timey 1960s bike movie, watching all the ridin' action in front of us.

And if there happens to be any Big Bumps in the upcoming road situation, we could tell by watching the bikes in front of us, then we'd know it was coming and we could brace for it. And speakin' of hittin' the Big Bumps, there are two kinds that really piss me off. First, there's the kind that sticks up, like a fuckin' speed bump, that knocks you up in the air, right? And then there's the other kind, the pot hole kind that you fall into and jars the shit outta your spine. I fuckin' hate both them fuckin' fuckers. And on this part of the ride, somehow, after pullin' outta the last gas station, Dave and me wound up in the front with a string of bikes behind us. And that's yet another weird goofy part of this Cursed 1988 Redwood Run. So we're are all nice and buzzed, gas tanks full, toolin' along 60 mph or so up Highway 101 with the pack behind us. Then all of a sudden.......

WHAM! Dave and me both hit this fuckin' speed bump thing that knocked us both up in the air sooo fuckin' high I thought we'd land our butts back down in San Jose, hahaha. We both yelled out FUCK! at the same time. I landed kinda on the top of the back of the front seat, feet kinda knocked off the pegs, Rat Chop wobblin' like Dave's 67 was, and I was still barely hangin' onto the drag bars,....when,....it happened.

WHAM! Again! After we landed on our seats, then here comes this second pot hole type of bump that we fell into and it jarred our spines soooo fuckin' hard that I thought my tail bone was gonna come up through the top of my haid, hahaha! DOUBLE FUCK! It hurt. 34 years ago and it still hurts, hahaha. But then another weird thing happened. We rounded a big bend in the road and laid out right before us was miles and miles of fresh new black top asphalt, so the Chopper Gods rewarded us with a smooth ride the rest of the way, after they nearly kilt us daid out on the road. But we hung in there. And then? Lookie here, we finally made it.

Our little group of San Francisco scooter trash finally made it to French's Campground, yay! But,...is the 1988 Redwood Run Curse lifted yet? Apparently not. It continues, and in a really horrible way. First the 'nearly got no weed' part, then the late Blabbermouth Corporate Start, then the flat tire at the Mom & Pop lunch joint, then the Two Huge-est Fuckin' Bumps in the World part, and what's next? Does the sky fall down on us?

We got here to French's and Dave on his 67 Old Yellow reaches into his jacket pocket to pull out his Redwood Run ticket,...which he still had in there. But,.....guess what else was now gone?

If you guessed Dave's brand spankin' new 1/2 ounce Zip Lock Baggie of Mendocino's Finest Skunk Weed is gone, then you are a winner! Oh nooooooooooo, Mister Bill. That's right. Dave forgot to zip up his pocket and while we were ridin' up the highway, somewhere, somehow, that big fluffy baggie fell outta his pocket and now it is gone. And I told Dave back then that I'd bet him a cold frosty Miller beer that his weed flew out when we hit them two fuckin' bumps. For havin' them shitty roads, the State of California owes Dave a 1/2 ounce of good weed, still today. I hope somebody found that baggie and put that awesome stinky shit to good use. I'd hate to think a cow ate it.

As if the 200 clams for the now-gone-weed wasn't bad enough to lose, this now means we only got half as much weed as we started out with.

So what's a decent guy to do? We found some aluminum foil in a trash can that probably came offa some eaten-up hot dog, I'm guessin', and I yanked out my weed and gave Dave half of it. At first he said no, for me to keep my weed. But then I said "What the fuck? You are gonna be smokin' it anyhow, so keep half of this on you. Besides,...that way if I get busted with it, they only catch me with half as much, hahaha." So Dave finally took it.

OK, now if ya look kinda close at the ground right underneath the 74 Rat Chop, you can see where it's marking its turf. When I say the poor ol' thing was rattin' out, I mean it was rattin' out, the once glorious show bike is turning into this oil slingin' kinda smoke-ie exhaust pipes type of mess, if ya know what I mean? How much longer will it hold together? We'll see. But first, we gotta get our wristbands and ride down into The Pit and pick out our spots before everybody else gets there and then we gotta set up them tents fast for the weekend's fun times.

Part 120: The California Rat Years

Continuing the Goofy 1988 Redwood Run

Our little band of scooter folks rode our 'sickles over the familiar bridge and down into The Pit and got us some really nice tent spots,.....in the hard dirt. Kinda close to the river, so not too bad. And once we got the tents set up, I thought all the weird shit was over. And then I looked up at the sky and saw this weird shit, I didn't know if it would show up on film or not, but I took it anyhow. And then when I got the film developed the next Monday, there it was. A weird Redwood Run Rainbow and there weren't no rain at the time, hadn't rained just before this photo and didn't rain after the photo. It just,........................'happened.'

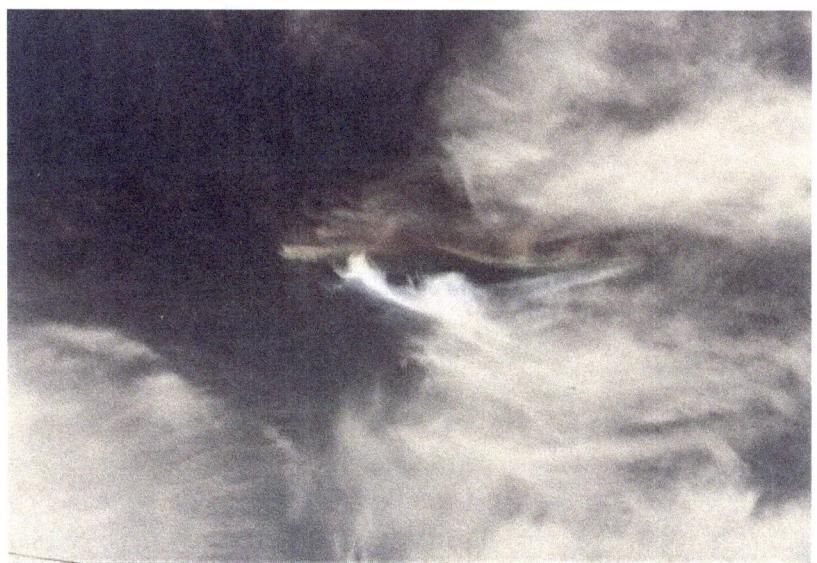

Part 121: The California Rat Years

Cursed & Weird 1988 Redwood Run

OK, not meaning to re-hash all the fuckin' misery, but here's all the weirdness that we got goin' on this Cursed & Weird 1988 Redwood Run,... so far. We had the 'no weed scare', the late corporate start, the flat tire, the two big bumps, Dave losin' his 1/2 ounce bag of weed, the weird colored formations in the sky that weren't a rainbow, and then the curse continues. And so far, this is all in the first day. It's still only Friday. Yikes!

Your ticket for the Redwood Run includes a steak dinner on Saturday night, but it don't do shit for you on Friday night. Friday nights you are on your own. So you can do a hot dog or burger from the food vendors,... if they are open for bid-ness. Or maybe you can grab a fish outta the river if you are really fast, or eat a squirrel if you can catch one. Or,...

................you can hop your stoned and/or drunk ass on your motorsickle and go for a nice little ride into town and see what you can scare up there? Kent & Lori and Dave and me decided to try the last option. We somehow thought we could take a chance and simply ride into town to find vittels,...on this cursed Redwood Run,...and not have any issues. Was that a good idea? What do you think? What could possibly happen now? Isn't our run of bad luck up yet?

So as we're ridin' into town, here comes The Pigs and they pulled Dave over on Old Yellow. Being the good brother I am to Dave, I patiently sat on the 74 Rat Chop with the motor off, so's The Pigs can't hear that I ain't got no mufflers. See there? Even though I'm kinda wasted, I still know how to fool the dumb ol' coppers, hahaha. So I sat there on the Rat Chop while they made Poor Ol' Dave do all the crazy funny looney shit, like try to walk a straight line, touch his nose, and other Funny Drunk Tricks. What the fuck do The Pigs think they are doing? Starting up some new kinda motorsickle game we can do in The Pit, like the Slow Race, Weenie Bite, Balloon Toss, or what?

While Dave was busy shittin' his britches with the asshole cops, I pulled out the trusty ol' Canon AE-1 camera and took this shot of Dave havin' fun with The Pigs. I thought that if they threw Dave in the Slammer forever, I could at least give his ol' lady Barbara these pictures to remember his drunk and stoned ass by, see how fuckin' nice I am? Always lookin' out for my brothers of the road. And yes, I'da done the same for you, ...why not?

Part 122: The California Rat Years

1988 Redwood Run Saturday

Woke up in the tents Saturday morning with a bit of a cotton mouth and hangover but so what? That's the way it's supposed to be. Our little group came outta the tents like hungry zombies and moseyed on down to the food vendors and got us some pancakes and coffee, nice wake up breakfast. Then the partyin' started in again. That's what we're here to do,.....right? And our weed supply is still doin' OK even though Dave lost his 1/2 ounce baggie somewhere out on the road.

As you can probably tell, this scene here is in the middle of the action in The Pit. Here we've got Dave's Old Yellow 67, my Nasty Black Rat Chop and Kent & Lori's new Blue Bike lookin' at ya. And it was at this 1988 Redwood Run that my buddy Dave and me started noticing that there weren't that many choppers showing up anymore. Seemed like the new Evos were takin' over.

Part 123: The California Rat Years

1988 Redwood Run Saturday Slow Race

Well, I'll be danged, look who showed up to the 1988 Redwood Run with his new prototype custom bike and entered the Slow Race. We've got the Bay Area's very own Arlen Ness here for you younger folks that might not recognize him. And a few months after I took this photo of Arlen ridin' his newest bike, it was in the magazines. And no, he did not win the Slow Race, ahem. Even with that big wide back tire. I thought Arlen had a good chance, but some other Slow Poke beat him not gettin' to the finish line, hahaha. Get it? It's a Slow Race, you don't wanna get there first-ses. .

Part 124: The California Rat Years

1988 Redwood Run Various Scenes

Easyriders Magazine crew showed up and we also have a photo here of the right side of French's Campground and another contestant in the Slow Race. And this guy was in a Facebook group once when I posted this photo an he said "Holy shit, that's me!" I think he said he was from Tacoma Washington and rode down to the Redwood Run.

And next he posted a photo of him on this very same bike and it was really him, see how that works? Eventually, I am gonna show a photo of every person in the USA that ever rode a bike to a Redwood Run. Well,...I guess that's kinda wishful thinkin' but who knows, you might see you in here next, wink, wink.

Part 125: The California Rat Years

1988 Redwood 'Nuther Beer Run

I know, I know,...... it's only a hunnerd yards or so over to the gawddamn beer tent, and I know most folks usually walked over to it, but this IS the Redwood Run and you ARE supposed to be ridin' Harleys in it. So whenever our dry hot thirsty crew would get a little bit low on the suds supply, I enjoyed kickin' over the Back Rat Chop and ridin' al.....l the way over there to the tent to get 'em.

Now, ya might wonder how or what am I gonna haul them cold frosty beers in? Glad you didn't ask. Here goes. If you've been payin' ultra close attention to all this garbage I been printin' up here on this old typewriter with the ribbon goin' bad, ya mighta noticed that whenever you see a picture of me with a beer, it usually ain't just one beer. If ya look close at them old pictures, there's usually 2 or 3 or 4 more beers a-hangin' on my handlebars.

We liked to drink cold beer. Lots of it. Gallons of it. Most of the time I'd get just two 6 Packs at once, so I wouldn't appear to be hoggin' it all up from everybody else, see? And I'd pull one nice cold beer outta each one of the 6 Packs. Then I'd take the empty spot that had that little plastic loop thing on the carryin' doo-dad, and I'd simply loop the plastic loop over each handlebar. See how good that works? It's downright simple.

Now I ain't claimin' that you could do this in your own town ridin' back from your own awesome beer store, but out here in The Pit, goin' only a hunnerd yards or so, that handlebar trick worked just fine. And lemme tell ya, I had it down to a science cuz we drank a few of them sudsy beers out there in the dirt over the years. And ya might be thinkin', wait a dang minnit. If he's all drunk and high an' shit, how's he gonna ride that suicide clutch and stift shift chopper and haul them beers on the handlebars all at the same time. The answer my friend,..is,....practice. Lots of practice.

Ok so now yer probably wonderin' what the hell did I do with them other two beers I pulled outta the 6 Pack? Well, I'd tuck my t shirt tail down inside the Levis and then drop the two beers down inside the neck hole, and I'd carry 'em like a mama 'possum or kangaroo. And the cold beer felt good inside. Like free air conditioning. OK and if ya notice the back rim on the Rat Chop in this photo. It ain't shiny.

Yep, it is a chrome rim, but it ain't shiny cuz it's covered in,.....umm,.....oil. When I say the Rat Chop was an nasty ol' oil slingin' rat at this stage, I ain't just a-whistlin' Dixie. But at least when yer Rat is covered in oil, it don't rust none. Them guys lookin' at me takin' off here were our campin' neighbors and they might be wonderin' if I'ma gonna fall over or not cuz they know how much I been drinkin'. Well, I never did fall over.

Part 126: The California Rat Years

1988 Redwood "Who is This Garberville Kid?"

Who is this Garberville kid? Is he you? Is he your kid, your grandkid, your cuzzin or nephew, or maybe your son in law today? Here is where this goofy-assed 1988 Redwood Run gets even goofier-assed. I don't even really know how to start this part of the story cuz it's soo fuckin' goofy. But since the California Statute of Limitations is up by now, so here we go. You might wanna grab a cup of coffee, a beer, a joint, or Jack & Coke for this next goofy part.

After the beer run I'd just made on the Rat Chop getting two more 6 Packs, I was hangin' out by our tents and bikes just kickin' back. Suddenly outta nowhere, up pops this kid in the red shirt and he's got two buddies with him. One guy is taller and looked kinda like David Lee Roth, the other kid was shorter and looked kinda like Dennis the Menace,...if you're old enough to remember him. I'm just guessin' they were around 14 years old or so?

At big runs like this, you kinda have your own 'neighborhood' where your tents and bikes are. Then you got other folks camped around you, maybe some people you remember from the year before, maybe you're meetin' some new friends. And some of those other camp sites can get pretty large, like 3 or 4 tents and maybe they have those nice tarp things set up on four sticks and they create their own shaded general hangout spot, which is really cool. What I'm gettin' at is, somtimes there's a few kids runnin' around the campground, and one time there was even a kid born at the Redwood Run pretty close to us. So I never gave it a second thought when these three little punkie kids came into our area.

Red Shirt Kid seemed to be their gang leader and he did most of the talkin'. They started in asking me questions about the Rat Chop. Typical shit, 'Are those funny shaped pipes loud? What is that belt thing on there? How do you work the clutch pedal, is it like a car's? What is that thing? How do you shift it?' Just regular run of the mill questions like that. As for the pipes? I said I'd start it up for them so they could hear it run. I turned the gas back on, hit the toggle switch, kicked it over and (luckily) it fired right up on the first kick,.....cuz it was already warm, hahaha.

Their eyes got pretty big and they started laughing. Then Red Shirt Kid asked if he could work the throttle some. Hmm. Normally I'da probably said no, but I was buzzed and havin' fun, and I flashed back to rememberin' what it was like bein' 14 or so,...so I said OK, go for it, but just don't overdo it. He grabbed the throttle and juiced it some, then the other two kids did, and then I shut it off. At this point I was expecting them to say 'thanks' or 'that was pretty cool' and go on about their merry little way. But they didn't. They kept standing there. And then I noticed them little fuckers were staring at my beer stash sitting in the shade by the tent. Then they asked me if they could have some beer. Gasp! What?

I said "You guys ain't old enough to be drinkin' that nasty cold beer. Where's your folks, anyhow? Where are you guys camped out at?" They said they were not camped out at the run and their folks were not there. They said their parents were back home in Garberville where they lived. Hmm,...again. Then I noticed these kids did not have on the required wrist bands. So I asked them "If your folks ain't here, and if you ain't camped out here, how the hell didya get in here to The Pit?"

Red Shirt Kid laughs and sez "We come in here and go swimming in the river all the time. We just came in through the back way over there....." and he's pointing back at the far side of the river where it makes a bend down at the end of French's Campground. Well I guess they know their way around here pretty good, huh? Hahaha. Then he said that is their swimming hole back there. Hmm,...again. So I hatched up a plan. I said "Look, I know it is hot and dry and dusty here right now, and I know you guys would probably like a beer, but it is highly illegal for me to give you fellers some cold frosty beers. I could get into trouble for Contributing to the Delinquency of a Minor.,...or three minors."

They looked kinda dejected, like I had just let them down big time. Then I sez, "But,..... let's say I was to walk over there by my green and yeller tent and I wasn't lookin' and you guys happened to 'steal' some beers, I guess I couldn't do anything about it." So I took a few steps over to the tent and then the next thing I heard was three cans of beer poppin' their tops behind me.

I expected them kids to walk away with their beers at this point. But they didn't. They kept hangin' around asking more questions about the Rat Chop. Or well, I should say the Red Shirt Kid and the David Lee Roth kid asked the questions, their buddy didn't seem to be all that interested. Maybe he liked Hondas better. Red Shirt Kid said he thought the Rat Chop was the coolest bike at the run they had seen. I said "Oh c'mon, there's tons of bikes here way nicer than mine." But he said he liked the way the Rat Chop was set up. And that's when it dawned on me that we might just have a future chopper builder here in our midst.

By this time, they had drained them beers, so they asked if they could steal some more. I laughed and said sure go for it but don't let me see you doing it. So they did. Now at this point, I was expecting them to go wandering away. But they didn't. Are they expectin' our group to adopt them for the weekend, hahaha? And then Red Shirt Kid reaches in his pocket and pulls out his joint case and grabs one out and he sez "Here, thanks for lettin' us steal your beers" and he tries to hand me the big fat joint. Gasp, again!

I sez "What the hell are you tryin' to do? That weed stuff is illegal, are you trying to Contribute to the Delinquency of an Adult? I can't take that from you. But maybe if I turned around and then found it sittin' there on the chopper's seat, then I guess I could fire it up." So I turned around for maybe 5 seconds, then when I looked back at the Rat Chop, there was a big fat joint from Garberville sittin' on the seat. And since

I did not actually see who put it there, the coppers and lawyers can not question me in court, cuz I don't know nuthin' about it at all, see?

So I called Dave and Kent & Lori over and I pulled out my trusty Zippo I've had since 1969 and I fired that fat Garberville joint up. And then, just as I have always done when some nice person offers me a joint to be lit and shared, I may or may not have given it back to Red Shirt Kid for him to maybe or maybe not pass around to his buddies and the rest of our group. And then,...this is the part where I expected the three kids to walk away, and they finally did. But it won't be the last we see of them. They were ruthless little punks out for a howlin'good time. You won't believe what they did later. I know I didn't. But meanwhile, we got the rest of the Redwood Run to enjoy. I think it was Lori who took this picture. And that kool-ass Armadillo ridin' a Chopper T shirt I got on is from Brown's Custom Cycle in Dallas.

Part 127: The California Rat Years

1988 Redwood, Movin' On Along...

So after we got them 3 teenage pot smokin' thugs to skee-dad-dle on along, Dave and Kent & Lori and me started off on our own to take in the motorsickle festivities in The Pit. Next, Dave borrowed Kent's ol' lady Lori,......and,......NO! Not that! Get your filthy mind outta the sex pervert gutter. He didn't borrow her to do The Big Nasty. He borrowed Lori for the 3 Legged Race, and don't say nuthin' about Dave's third leg, neither. Sheeesh.

Anyhow, in the 3 Legged Race, they were doin' purdy good,...until they weren't. They tripped up and went down in a big cloud of The Pit Dust. But they were in Second Place until they crashed. Better luck next time. This is them just after Dave helped Lori back up,...just after Dave made Lori fall down. Good thing I was there with the camera to catch the action, eh? And the couple that WAS in First Place,......also crashed and burned.

Then our little stoned out rag-tag group wandered over to the area with the Balloon Toss, an old Redwood Run tradition from way back in the late 1970s,...they tell me, anyhow. And the best thing about the Balloon Toss is the gals sometimes miss the water balloons and then them balloons pop up against the gals' breats-ses-ses, see? So it kinda ends up like a Wet T-Shirt Contest, hahaha.

And next we meandered over to the Weenie Bite contest. This is Lori right here in the pink shirt bitin' the mustard coated weenie while she is perched on Kent's New Blue Machine. We watched the gals on back of the Harleys bite and suck on the weenies for a while, then we headed off to other parts of The Pit.

Part 128: The California Rat Years

1988 Redwood, Where's Da Weed?

Next up on the agenda, since the Three Garberville River Rat Kids had told me about a good swimmin' spot down at the end of French's Campground, and since I was an Old Icicle River Rat that likes swimmin' in rivers better than I like swimmin' in swimmin' pools or lakes, I decided to hoof it on down to the corner bend in the river to see what them thuggy kids were gabbin' about. I tried to get Kent or Lori or Dave to go with me, but I think they were afraid of gettin' wet, like they might shrink or somethin'. And since I hadn't had no shower in a spell and since it was kinda hot, dry and dusty, I decided so..... what the hell? I'm gonna go swimmin'.

I got up to the corner where they said the swimmin' hole was, and there it was, a perfect place just like they had described. So I yanked my 1977 Easyriders Magazine Nasty Feet boots and socks off, pulled off my belt, wallet and keys, and I jumped in the river with all the rest of my duds on, cuz they could use a freshen up as well. Right? Right. It was a great swimmin' spot and the current was just perfect, not too much to drag you away, but enough to feel good, kinda like you were flying around in the sky if you swam against the current.

Then I got ready to go back to camp. Got outta the water, put my socks and boots back on, got my wallet, belt and keys, and headed on back to our tent area. Then when I got back to the folks there, I decided it was time for another nice big fat Mendocino stick. And then I reached into my pocket and..........................uh oh.

No weed! FUCK!

My weed was gone. That means we started out on the Redwood Run with a nice fluffy full ounce, Dave had lost his half on the road to the Highway & Wind Gods, so I'd given him half of what I had left, and now my baggie is gone! Oh shit. So I broke the horrible news to Dave, Kent & Lori, and we immediately set out on an Emergency Search & Rescue Mission.

We re-traced all my steps out to the swimmin' hole at the end of the bend in the river. Why did them damn kids hafta tell me about that shit? Normally, I'da just jumped in the river right here where our tents were, my old familiar spot. But noooooo, I had to go try out a new spot and now the weed baggie is in gones-ville. Damn and double damn!

We searched and searched in the rocks. To those of you reading this that know the area in The Pit that I'm blabbin' about, you know how rough and rocky that spot is down there. There were millions of holes in the rocks where the weed could have fallen and got swallered up, never to be seen again,...or smoked. This was like lookin' for a needle in the haystack, for real.

And then? Lori yells out, "I FOUND IT!" She is now my hero of all times, Since we had the camera with us, Dave took this one of Lori and me with the baggie she found. Whew!

Part 129: The California Rat Years

1988 Redwood, Wet T-Shirt Contest

Ya can't have a goofy fun Redwood Run without a Wet T-Shirt Contest,...right? I think so. I figgered nobody would be all that interested in seeing a bunch of little wet skimpy T-Shirts cuz you can see them at home in your washing machine any ol' time. So I thought I'd just skip to the good part where the gals took 'em off. Hope you don't mind too much. This gal here was the winner. I wonder why? She ain't even got her Wet T-Shirt on?

Part 130: The California Rat Years

1988 Redwood, Campground Shot

For this panorama shot I took the Canon camera and held it as still as I could in my drunken paws to snap the picture of the left side of the campground and shot the first photo on the left. Then I panned over to the right side of the campground and lined up the left side of the frame with the same trees and bikes as before, then took that shot.

Now back in them 35 mm film days, we had no idea what happened with the result of a photo attempt like this until we got the photos back from the camera shop. And in this case, it turned out pretty damn good, especially for a drunk bum like me taking it.

Part 131: The California Rat Years

1988 Redwood, Shots out on the Road

These photos here are of the action right at the Main Entrance of French's Campground. Kinda crowded, huh? Not a whole lotta home built choppers left at the runs like there used to be. We got two photos of a big pile of bikes and then there's one with Kent & Lori.

Part 132: The California Rat Years

1988 Redwood, Various Bike Shots

Here's some shots of the different types of Harleys that showed up for the 1988 Redwood Run. We got a crazy Three Wheeler here, except it's actually a Five Wheeler, hahaha. And then a coupla nice choppers, one on the classic side and one on the kinda krazy side, and you can be the judge of which one is which.

Part 133: The California Rat Years

1988 Redwood, Steaks, Elvin, & Acid

I always liked climbin' up on the big hill in back of the The Pit and taking in the view and excitement from up on top. There was usually a nice breeze up there and it was fun times listenin' to all the Harley motors runnin' down below. And it always got a little bit excitin' when we saw the smoke fire up down in The Pit, cuz that meant they were firin' up the grills for them nice juicy steaks we'd eat in the dirt and wash down with suds.

In one other photo scene here in The Pit, I was just shootin' a photo of the crowd in general. And then when I got home and got the pictures developed, lookie who's sneakin' in the left side of the frame, hahaha. Yep, there's Red Shirt Kid again with his shaggy buddy. What the hell are they still doing there?

After Dave, Kent & Lori and me were done eaten them steaks, I walked back over to my tent and the Rat Chop and was puttin' in another roll of film, gettin' ready to go watch the Elvin Bishop Band. And who do ya think I ran into at my tent? If you guessed Red Shirt Kid was there again, you are 100% correct. But this time he wasn't lookin' fer any free beer to steal. This time he was grinnin' like crazy, and I was wonderin' what was up?

That kool little guy stuck out his paw to shake hands, so I did. Then he said "Thanks for the beer today, I really appreciated it. Here ya go." And he held out his other hand toward me. I had no idea what he meant, he just kept grinnin' that big possum grin. Then he said again "Here, take this." And when I looked down, that Red Shirt Kid gave me a hit of blotter. So THAT'S why he's grinnin' sooooo fuckin' big. I told him thanks and stuck it under my tongue, so here we go now, trippin' to Elvin Bishop Band, and then after they were done, the Marshall Tucker Band came on stage.

Part 134: The California Rat Years

1988 Redwood Run Trippin'

So Red Shirt Kid's hit of blotter took off pretty good, hahaha. I got them funny butterflies in my belly and started grinnin' and laughin' like hell. A little while later I caught up with Dave and Kent & Lori and they kept asking me what's so fuckin' funny? I kept laughin' and said "Oh,...nuthin' really. Just trippin' on the acid that the Red Shirt Kid gave me".....

When they were askin' how come I got some free acid and they didn't, I said "You shoulda let them thuggy kids steal some beers from you while you weren't lookin' and then you'd have some...maybe. Or maybe he gave me some cuz he said he liked my Rat Chop the best?"

Who knows? What I do know is I took this one crummy picture of the 74 Rat Chop in The Pit while I was Flyin' High on the good stuff. And this one here actually turned out to be one of my favorite photos of this entire run. Not just cuz I was trippin', but becuz this picture here has an extra special seedy gritty quality to it. If this one picture here don't totally sum up "The Pit" then I don't know what does, wink, wink.

Part 135: The California Rat Years

1988 Redwood, Marshall Tucker Band

It's been a wild and crazy Redwood Run so far, the goofiest one ever for me. Just one crazy mindfuck after another after another after another mindfuck. First our late start, then my flat tire, and Dave's lost weed, then my lost weed, and now some free and unexpected trippin' on blotter. What more could ya ask for?

So now it has come down to this. It's Saturday Night, which is Fun Night. My belly's fulla steak and beer with some Acid thrown on top, and we still got lots of weed left, so that's good. I'm trippin' just wanderin' around the campground. Been seein' people and bikes and saw the Elvin Bishop Band. And now it's time for the Main Event, Mister Marshall Tucker.

Imagine bein' all this fucked up, laughin your ass off and feelin' this good and then ya got Marshall Tucker playin' right in front of you? Yep, that's exactly how it happened.

Part 136: The California Rat Years

1988 Redwood, The Mornin' After

Oh man, hahaha. Sunday mornin' I opened my eyes and was happy to discover I had gotten my trippin' & laughin' ass back inside the tent, and it was even my tent, so that was good. All my ears was ringin' from the Marshall Tucker Band,...so that was also good. I stared up at the yellow tent roof wonderin' if I could move and get up and get around to meet the new day. There wasn't all that much racket outside yet, so it musta still been kinda early.

Normally at this juncture, I'd be pullin' on my Easyriders Nasty Feet boots, but I didn't hafta do that this morn cuz they were still on. Good. That saves me the time of lacin' up them 6 foot long boot laces, cuz the tops of them steel toed and steel shanked boots come nearly up to your knee. And I still got all my clothes on, so that was extra good. That means even though I was all high and trippin' and drunk, at least I wasn't runnin' around the campground nekked as a jay bird like I had seen other drunken souls do before, how em-bare-ass-kin'. -Popeye

I was still a-layin' there on my back, looking up at the tent roof, then I reached over with my left hand to wipe the sandy gritty dirt shit outta my eyeball holes. And when I let my left hand back down,...... WHACK! The back of my hand landed right on the pointy spike nut on the top of the Rat Chop's front fender. Ouch, gawddammit! Now some of you might wonder what the hell was the front fender doin' inside the tent? And others of you who might be very observant mighta coulda noticed that sometimes in these run photos, the front fender is on the Rat Chop and sometimes it is off. Why is that?

Cuz I'd have the fender mounted on the bike when we were ridin' up to the run, and I'd have it on there ridin' home from the run. I ran the fender cuz I did not want the road gear slippin' down onto the bare front tire, see? But while we were there in the campground, I'd pull it off so the Rat Chop would look more "chopperish",..... if ya get what I mean? So catchin' that pointy spike nut on the back of my hand was a good wake up call. Nuthin' like some pain first thing in the mornin' to get ya goin', right?

I sat up, crossed my legs, grabbed the baggie and rolled up a nice big fat joint of the fresh Mendocino Sticky Shit. When I'm kinda in a hungover-type mood, what I do not want first thing in the morning is to be takin' a drag off some old stale roach that was left over from the night before. I want some fresh stuff. So I rolled it and lit it and held it in to feel good. Then I finally drug my ass outta the tent to see if everybody else saw still alive, hahaha. They were. Good.

As I stood there stretchin', I noticed that the Canon camera was hangin' by its shoulder strap on the right side of the drag bars. Oooops! Left that sucker on there all night long. See there? Ain't it nice how honest them scooter trash folks can be? Why, if I'da been campin' with a bunch of cops or lawyers, they'da ripped off that camera for sure, hahaha.

Standing there beside the tent stretchin' and yawnin' some more, my foot knocked over a Miller Beer can and there was still some beer in it. Quick! Grab it, hah! Now maybe that was a beer I had been drinkin' on and maybe it was somebody else's can, but whoever's it was the night before, it was now mine this morning. I looked inside just to check if there was a ciggie butt in it, and there wasn't, so now it's fair game. Might sound sorta gross to those with weak bellies, but warm flat beer still solves the Dreaded Cotton Mouth Disease. I slugged down that brewski. Burp.

Now it's time to do what everybody in this type of condition must do. Go take a leak, dammit. I stumbled over to the stinky outhouses and did the natural thing. Then I took this picture of the outhouse hole, just so's I could show it to you these 34 years later. Here's a coupla other shots of the campground and some folks with their bikes, which I took a litttle later in the day when everybody was wakin' up and movin' around some.

Part 137: The California Rat Years

1988 Redwood, Sunday Mornin' Gotta Eat

After the Kent & Lori and Dave Zombies all got up and were movin' around, we decided to ride into town and have ourselves a nice big wake up breakfast before all the rest of the Redwood Run Horde got up and made the same damn plans, haha. So we're just blastin' down the highway on the way to gobble us some breakfast and Kent & Lori were ridin' over to the side of me. I had no idea Lori was even takin' this picture right here.

But she did, and then they gave it to me a few days later when we all got together again. And that's how this 'Surprise Picture' has turned out to be one of my favorite mystery photos of the Rat Chop over the last 48 years ridin' on it. And there's them big Nasty Feet boots and a wild bunch of hair that musta blown out on the road over the past few years. Lemme know if ya find it, wink, wink. Dang, I sure miss all them good California people and them fun California Rat Years days.

Part 138: The California Rat Years

1988 Redwood Run Sunday Fun

Well it's gettin' closer to the Sad Time, the time we gotta pull our camp spot apart and load up the bikes for the return ride back home. But first, here's a coupla other shots. We got the Iron Horses lined up, and I'm guessin' this is at the Breakfast Grub Corral? And then if ya remember back to the very beginning of this Redwood Run Kick Off, there was that nice lookin' gal in the black leather outfit in the parking lot with the trees? Well I just found her again, and this time she's walking along with her guy in this Sunday mornin' camp ground photo.

Part 139: The California Rat Years

1988 Redwood Run, Ridin' Home

They say all good things must come to an end,...and so must the Goofy 1988 Redwood Run. I put the Rat Chop's front fender back on, 4 bolts and 4 spacers, can do it in less than 5 minutes with a 1/2 inch wrench. We pulled our tents down, rolled up our sleepin' bags and packed everything on the bikes.

Dave kicked his 67 Old Yellow Chopper over, I kicked over the 74 AMF Rat Chop and Lori jumped on back while Kent hit his new fangled starter button and we were off in a cloud of Pit Dust, ridin' in the dirt outta French's Campground headed out to the paved highway again. Once we were situated in a nice sized pack of Harleys rollin' south down 101, I kinda sat back in the Rat Chop saddle and thought about what a crazy run this had been.

My belly and face were still sore from all the laughin' from the night before on the blotter acid that them thuggie kids gave me. I still had Marshall Tucker songs ringin' in my ears in tune to the upsweep fishtails, puttin' along with my best ridin' buddies on my ol' crappy home built chopper with the suicide clutch and stick shift. All our exhaust pipes were singin' together in the wind. Yep it was a good fun run, even though we had "issues" along the way.

And then while we were rollin' down the highway, my mind started wandering back to my teenage years and to them kool little juvenile delinquent kids that had just crashed our camp site in The Pit,...for free. When I was 14 years old, it was 1969. That means the Easy Rider movie just came out and so did Then Came Bronson on the Boob Toob. 1969 and that movie and TV show changed my life forever, made me what I am today,...whatever that is, hahaha. And when I was 14,...these kids' age,...I thought I was kinda kool cuz I had ridden my bicycle over close to the Drive-In Movie Theater. I sat on my bicycle and watched Easy Rider for free from over the fence, even though I couldn't really hear it too good. And after I had done that, I told all my friends about it, thinkin' that was some purdy cool shit that I did.

Now,...let's compare what I did to what Red Shirt Kid and his two buddies did. First, they snuck into The Pit, which many adults get busted tryin' to do, but them kids made it happen for themselves cuz they knew the river better than anyone else did. Next, they got to twist the throttle on a 74 Stroker Rat Chopper. And then they got to drink beer they 'stole' from me whilst I wasn't lookin' and then they got to smoke lots of good weed. And last but not least, they were trippin' on acid and watching the Marshall Tucker Band playin' in The Pit.

Them three little thuggie kids got to do more fun illegal shit in one Saturday night than a lotta 50 year old adults have done in their entire lives. Think about that fer a second and let it sink in. My hat is off to them three kids, whoever they were, and where ever they are these days. Maybe they are reading this right now, who knows? They are probably in their late 40s or early 50s by now. Maybe Red Shirt Kid builds and rides nice choppers? Maybe he still remembers that funny Saturday night when he was trippin' down in The Pit?

Meanwhile, I remember suddenly without any warning, I hit a purdy good sized bump and it snapped my foggy noggin back to reality,...and then a little bit later we pulled off the highway for a gas stop and maybe a beer or three. This fine Knuckle Chopper was sittin' there, all packed up for the road. Can ya even begin to imagine how many knuckle-bustin' painstakin' hours went into this Creation of Love? Not to mention the mountain of cash it took? This is probably my favorite bike I saw on the entire run. Why, this Knuckle is soooo fuckin' purdy, I'da been too embarrassed to even think about parkin' the Rat Chop next to it.

Part 140: The California Rat Years

1988 Redwood Run, Over & Done

As we got closer and closer to the Bay Area, folks started splittin' off our group to head on down their own exits. Kent & Lori also took off for their exit. That left Dave and me on our two Shovel Chops ridin' on along together. Lot quieter now with just the two of us.

We rode on acrost the Golden Gate Bridge and into San Francisco. My stop was gonna be in the middle of the city, in The Haight. Dave still had to ride on south of the city for a bit, 15 minutes or so. But before we split up, we stopped and took this picture of our two Shovel Chops at the end of the run.

And little did we know this would be the last time these two versions of our trusty ol' Shovelheads would be photographed together. So this is it. The End of the 67 Old Yellow with the 74 Black Rat Chop,...sniff, sniff,.....and double sniff sniff. Dave will never ride the 67 Old Yellow next to the Black 74 Rat Chop again.

Part 141: The California Rat Years

End of June 1988 Leavin' California

The California Rat Years are comin' to a close at this stage. The city of San Francisco passed some kinda moratorium on new construction, like the city was getting too crowded and didn't want any newer buildings crowdin' up their skyline? And since I am in the sawdust-eatin' construction racket,...that meant here comes the job cuts for me.

On the flip side at work, the company I had been working for building the new Nordstroms store in downtown San Francisco was based in Seattle. And those nice Seattle boss guys offered me a job working for them in Seattle if we wanted to move up there. So,...what the fuck? Let's move to Seattle.

It ain't that far and I love Washington State and have some really good ridin' buddies up there anyhow. So now I'm gonna get to go see all my old pals from the Chopper Hobo days. This is one of the last photos taken from our Penthouse window up on top of Buena Vista West, in the Haight Ashbury. Gonna miss this place, for sure.

Part 142: The California Rat Years

End of June 1988: 64 Sting Ray Road Trip to Seattle

We threw a few clothes and tools in the 64 Sting Ray and headed off to find a new place to live in a new city neither one of us had lived in before. Although I'd lived a coupla years in Ellensburg and Wenatchee back in the early 1980s when I was still single, I didn't know a soul in Seattle.

So, we set out to find a cheapie apartment in Seattle, kinda close to downtown since that was where I'd be working most of the time. Seattle is kinda like San Francisco, a city of hills. And Queen Anne is the high dollar one, so that left us out. Up on top of Capitol Hill has a nice view and it's kinda close to downtown, but still kinda pricey. So we settled on a 1 bedroom on the lower side of Capitol Hill, which is kinda the scummy side. But.....the joint we were looking at as Prospect #1 had a swimmin' pool, so that was nice. And the most important part about this dump was it sat on the ground floor. That means I could roll the Rat Chop in and out of the apartment door.

We paid the first/last rent and deposit and left the Sting Ray sittin' in its new parking spot out right off the alley. No garage spot for it either, so that's bad. I'd gotten used to having a garage at the flat and Penthouse in Frisco. Now I'd hafta do without,...for a while, until I found one? If I was lucky? Anyhow, I wasn't really worrying about a garage for the Rat Chop cuz I had me some new plans for that critter.

And those plans included a brand new rebuild, from bare sandblasted frame back up, with the old pipe-welded up neck cut off and a new one custom built, plus new motor and tranny builds. And since we now ain't got no garage, that means the new 74 AMF Chopper will be built in the living room of a 1 bedroom apartment in Seattle, hahaha. Big deal, I used to build my choppers inside my house in Dallas, so I was used to that. Building choppers inside where you live is closer to the beer in the fridge anyhow, right?

This is the last photo of our old apartment building up on the hill in the Haight. And this is Mister Bruce Southard, our Building Manager. Him and his wife Kay were sooo ultra cool. Bruce served under Patton in WW 2 over in Germany. So when I asked him if I could take one last picture of him on the roof of his building entrance, he gave me his Best Heil Hitler Salute. And now you get to see it, all these 34 years later.

Part 143: The California Rat Years

July 1988, California Rat Years is Over

After we paid down on the scummy 1 bedroom apartment on the lower west side of Capitol Hill and left the 64 Sting Ray sittin' in its parking spot, we grabbed our sleepin' bags and duffel bags fulla clothes and we hopped our butts on the Green Tortoise Bus back to San Francisco. What the hell is a Green Tortoise Bus? A bunch of old hippies from San Francisco bought a few old used SF Muni buses from the city. And then they went into business riding folks up and down the west coast for a cheaper price than Greyhound did.

Green Tortoise buses were set up like diners and sleeper cars in trains, back when we had nice old trains with sleeper cars. Inside the bus during the daytime, instead of having seats where you stare at the back of the person's noggin in front of you, the Green Tortoise buses had booths set up, tables for 4 all up and down the bus. You could play cards, checkers, dominoes, read a book, listen to your Walkman headphones, whatever you wanted to do.

AND,.....and you could also bring along your own cassette tapes and the bus driver would play everybody's music while you're going down the highway. It was a party bus and a really fun way to travel. You got to meet new folks who were very interesting, to me, anyhow. The Green Tortoise company also owned land in the middle of Oregon. They had a big hippie camp with tee pees set up out in the middle of the woods on the cleanest river in the state, and Oregon has some clean rivers, or they did back then. So the bus would stop at their hippie camp out in the woods and that's where you'd eat.

Half the people on the bus would help cook the meal and the other half,.....us,....helped clean up afterward. They had awesome food out there in the woods, fresh fish just yanked outta the river, shredded pork shoulder, roast beef, grilled chicken, and all kinds of salads. Oh,...and the hippie guys' moms also lived out there and they'd bake the fresh pies, cherry, apple, blueberry, and olallieberry pies,...that's a delicious Oregon pie and ya probably won't find them olallieberries anywhere else. While the bus riders would be cookin' and eatin' and cleanin' the dishes, the hippie bus crew would be busy converting the booth/tables into sleepers. Just like in a regular camper, they'd drop the table top down to where it made a bed.

Now, this might sound all fine and dandy to you. And it did to me, except for one funny thing that happened when this younger long hair guy got on the bus with his 40 ouncer of Miller Beer. 40 ounces of beer is like 5 of those 8 ounce Coke bottles from when I was a kid. That's quite a bit of beer to be swillin' really fast. And what happens when ya drink a lotta beer? Didya catch the part about where the hippies made their buses outta the San Francisco Muni buses? Do ya get the difference between a city bus and a Greyhound bus?

Answer: City buses ain't got no bathrooms in the back section, our bus driver was sort of a kooky spiky haired Lez-bean gal, fulla tats and face piercings. She ain't got no sense of humor, either, ya might say. She was all bid-ness. And this long haired guy suddenly had to take a leak really bad. (Big surprise?) We were sittin' up kinda close to the front and got to witness this action. The guy leans over to the bus gal and tells her he's gotta take a leak. She tells him he shoulda done that at the last bus stop. (Cuz this bus does make regular stops along the way at bus stations to pick folks up and let folks off, see?) So the guy tells the gal drivin' the bus "Well I didn't hafta piss back then, but I do now!"

And here's the funny part. WIthout missin' a beat, the bus gal suddenly points her right hand with the cut off fingerless glove over toward the bus door and she shakes her pointer finger at the funnel hanging there. And this funnel is mounted to the bus's entry door jamb with a water hose attached to the bottom of the funnel and it's going out the door, BWAHAHAHA! So in front of all the passengers on the bus,...maybe 25 or 30 people?,...this poor 40 Ouncer Miller Beer guy has to unzip his britches and pull his tallywhacker out and pee right in front of everybody, hahaha, with the drain hose sprayin' all the pee down the road behind us. How would ya like to be ridin' your motorcycle behind that spray, thinkin' it's stinky rain? I mean, what buses go down the road sprayin' piss all over the place? But hey, at least he didn't hafta take a crap,...right? Yikes!

We finally made it back to San Francisco. I went down to U Haul and got a truck. Then I rode the 74 Rat Chop up inside the truck and tied it off. And yes, for those of you who have been following all this drivel for a long time, you might notice this is the first time I ever hauled the 74 AMF Chop anywhere. I always rode it to where I was movin',...but that was back when I was single and umm,...free. Now I'm all hitched up an' shit. So we loaded the rest of the stuff from the little Penthouse into the U Haul and took off up north up Highways 1 and 101, enjoying the coast all the way up to the Pacific Northwest, our new home.

And when we got to Seattle to the new 1 bedroom scummy dump, guess what had happened while we were gone? If you guessed some rotten low life scum bag muthafucker stole the hubcaps off the 64 Sting Ray whilst we were in California, then you are correct. Here's our new Seattle home town, and this shot was taken from over in West Seattle, with the hubcaps stolen.

Part 144: The California Rat Years

July 1988, Landin' in Seattle,...With a Thud

Well folks, we have finally reached the end of the morbid California Rat Years. I'm about outta typewriter paper and this typewriter ribbon is nearly bone dry, I can just barely see what it even sez. So while you go out and have some fun doin' what you like to do when nobody's lookin', I'll do a big ol' puff and then run down to the corner drug store and hop up on a counter stool and have a nice big greezy bacon cheeseburger with fries and a chocolate shake, and I want them to leave that big stainless steel cup with the extra shake in it. And then I'll grab me some more typewriter paper and a fresh new typewriter ribbon, and I'll start typin' up the next part of the Sordid Saga for you, that is, if you can stand any more.

Here's five last photos for you. The U Haul truck is packed leavin' the Haight for Seattle. Then we got the new underground basement scummy apartment we moved into, and then a shot of the swimmin' pool and you can see downtown whilst yer swimmin'. Then there's one more of them double photo things I do sometimes, where I took two pictures and stuck 'em together for a panoramic view, and last and certainly least, we got the 74 Rat Chop parked just outside our glass window, and,............WHOA!

What the fuck are them muffler things doing on there? I've never run mufflers in my life! Have I gone crazy and flipped out? Did you put those on there while I wasn't lookin'? Next up on the plate we will rebuild the smoky old oil slingin' and drippin' 74 Rat Chop into the semi-beautiful show winning chopper that will eventually get a 6 page spread in Easyriders and V Twin magazines. And yes, of course there will be another catastrophic fire, the worst fire yet this time, with burnt up motor parts and lost tranny parts, and movin' from three different apartments in two different states in less than two years, and lots of painful gut wrenchin' misery involved that makes me wanna blow chunks just thinkin' about it all. Yikes.

Oh, and that Seattle based company I was working for in San Francisco building up that Nordstroms store that told me they had a job waiting for me in Seattle? Nope, hahaha. That fell through. When I went to their main office to go to work for them, they told me just because one of our Superintendents down in California said you could go to work here doesn't mean we have a spot for you. We have our own guys on layoff right now. Hmm. I said "I am one of your own guys" and pulled out the little company card that had my employee ID number on it.

Ummm,...no dice. Bye. Don't let the door hit ya in the ass on the way out.

So now we're stuck in Seattle in a scumbag underground apartment, no job, the Rat Chop is falling apart, and the hubcaps are stolen off the Sting Ray. Oh well, at least we had a swimmin' pool at the dump, what more could ya ask for?

To see the upcoming photos and dreadful stories of all that horrible burned up Seattle fuck-mess, you'll hafta tune in next time, Same Rat Time, Same Rat Channel.

The End

Books in this series by Shovelhead Dave

Available in paperback or eBook online on Amazon and most leading bookshops worldwide.

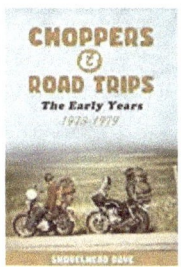

The First Book 1973-1979. Shovelhead Daves first bikes and road trips. Made an Amazon No 1 in only 4 days after release.

The Second book 1979 to 1983 Dave becomes a Homeless Hobo living in the woods with his Chopper Bike

California Rat Chopper Years. The Third book 1983 to 1988

Rat Chopper to Show Chopper coming in 2023

A final word from the Editor and a great Recommendation.

Like a lot of people who start out on two wheels as their first form of transport, I progressed onto cars, starting a business, marriage, kids and so on the motorcycling got forgotten and left behind as a mode of transport and adventure until I hit my 50s……a strange time in life when 50 hits you and you realise maybe your best years are behind you and what am I going to do now?....so one day whilst reflecting on my past and remembering those days of being young and free behind the bars of a bike, a lifelong friend of mine from those years and who was still riding and doing various bike adventures worldwide told me to get back on a bike and be free so, I brought his KTM 1190R Adventure bike.

Now that thing was a rocket ship at 160BHP and great fun…. I rode it with him and another guy from the UK to Amsterdam in 12 hrs to a vintage Harley meeting of all things…. my two buddies Quintin and Steve had the KTM 1290 Adventure bikes and rode in racing competitions, they rode fast all the way so I had to keep up…. I hadn't really rode murder-cycles for 30 years other than having a quick go on my younger brother's deathtrap chopper… (which never legally made it onto the roads….just as well….)

So, the KTM was a bit too fast for my liking, a bucking bronco… kinda like a baptism of fire introduction back into motorcycling however maybe a bit too much bike for my age and what I was seeking out of motorcycling, at some point in the future I was going to kill myself on that thing……besides I always wanted a Harley Right? Nothing sounds like a Harley…..

So I got one, then two then three….. you know how it goes…. I started collecting a few……then too many became garage queens as nice as it is to own such fine machines I realized just doing a few "local rides" shows and bike nights as a part time biker just wasn't giving me that great feeling I had all those years ago out there on a bike riding new roads to places I hadn't been to before, and each ride was an adventure in its own way.

Until one day my motorcycle racing friends told me about a trip they were doing in India riding the foothills of the Himalaya's for two weeks on Royal Enfield 500s...... ah not rocket ships I thought....I can do that and I love the mountains and a chance to ride the Himalaya's? it was a no brainer... so I got the details from them, The India Motorcycle Tour company, you want some fun on a motorcycle again with like minded people or with your mates as a group then try this company.

Yes yet again...another Baptism of fire... riding India's Roads with crazy sights you'd never see back home..... oh my word it was fun, two weeks of motorcycling adventures in a "new world" just like it was when we got that first taste of freedom on a bike without pedals, taking you out to places you've never been before with the wind in your face discovering the rest of the world outside of your life's bubble, and maybe even out of your regular comfort zone, just maybe a little bit like the young Shovelhead Dave felt at the time.

Now some of you are old school lifelong bikers reading these books for enjoyment and some of you may read these books to feel that spirit of Adventure, perhaps like me, some of you didn't live that lifetime of motorcycling fun and experience's that Shovelhead Dave writes about, and maybe have returned to it in our later years.

I know the world has changed since, however.... whatever bike you ride or genre of biking you do or follow, riding India still offers those adventures discovering new places and culture in a developing country with many parts still in an old timey world where time has almost stood still, modern against old all-in co-existence of each other and working, and at the same time riding and seeing some fantastic sights, some may shock you some may wow you...

I have just completed my second trip in Sept 2022 with the India motorcycle tour company this time riding 10 of the world's highest motorable roads some at nearly 18,000 ft altitude and also crossing a high-altitude desert, riding 3000km over 15 days…. Yes, it was awesome, maybe I'll write about them in a book one day… Now you are thinking yeah right who am I going to do this with……. I'm too old….my mates don't ride anymore…. this time I went without my two mates because they had other commitments and met up with the other members of the new group for the first time at Delhi airport.

One of them being aged 72 and having previously done a ride 4 years ago with the same company in South India had overshot a corner and ended up in a farmer's field, he was unhurt and back riding after the others dragged his bike out… he returned for this trip because he had the time of his life on the last ride, but decided to do this one in a jeep this time following us and had just as much fun.

Considering this guy (Robin is his name) is an ex RAF navigator clocking up some 2500 hours in the Vulcan bomber during the cold war years you'd think he'd had enough excitement in his lifetime! a wonderful man with some great life experiences and stories, you can hear his testimonial on the India motorcycle Tour company website and he quotes "They say that flying is the sport of kings and motorcycling is the next closest thing and perhaps the sport of princes" ….you never know who you are going to meet on these trips but we all have a great laugh and we are all characters sharing the same spirit of adventure.

So, there is always that Jeep option, and you can bring the old lady too if you don't fancy busting your butt in the saddle anymore or the missus busting your butt about going on a trip without her, and as motorcyclists do, we still all look out for each other even if in a Jeep!

You want something different from cocktails on the beach? Maybe an item for the bucket list? Then ride and live adventures while you can... check them out on their website, **theindiamotorcycletourco.com** they will even tailor a ride to suit your times and trip length, fuel, bikes, hotels, food, back up truck following with mechanic with a guide leading the way all arranged and included, I'll be riding many more tours with them in 2023 so hopefully I'll get to meet some of you.

Keep on motorcycling live your dreams and make memories just like Shovelhead Dave!

Richard Sheehy Editor

P.s Don't forget to tell the India Motorcycle tour company you got this recommendation from me! and in true Shovelhead Dave style, take pictures on your trip .....Bwahahaha

Thought I'd stop for a Yak or two on a mountain road, I must have been missing the missus yammering on......

The Editor Richard Sheehy taking the Chopper Hobo Book to the world's highest motorable roads with the India Motorcycle Tour Co, on their Land of the High Passes Tour during Sept 2022.

The Royal Enfield's started protesting the last 400ft on this one due to the thin air, but made it up there just like the two Hondas going up Pikes Peak, Colorado, in Shovelhead Dave's First book "The Early Years"

Taking in the views with two of the riders on this trip Nigel Lilley and Tim Chapman, two fantastic guys I had the pleasure of riding with and having a great laugh throughout the whole adventure.

MAKE UNFORGETABLE MOTORCYCLE ADVENTURES OF A LIFETIME WITH

Website: www.theindiamotorcycletourco.com

Email: info@theindiamotorcycletourco.com

Phone: +91 9810 278859 Rajeev Bagga (Owner)

www.ingramcontent.com/pod-product-compliance
Lightning Source LLC
Chambersburg PA
CBHW050336230426
43663CB00010B/1879